macro magic for kids and Parents

Taking the mystery out of macrobiotic cooking

Sheri-Lynn DeMaris

Wilmington, Delaware

macro magic for Kids and Parents
Taking the mystery out of macrobiotic cooking

First Printing

Published by:
Cedar Tree Books, Ltd.
P.O. Box 4256
Wilmington, Delaware 19807
books@ctpress.com
www.cedartreebooks.com

ISBN 978-1-892142-45-0

Title: Macro Magic for Kids and Parents: Taking the Mystery Out of Macrobiotic Cooking
Author: Sheri-Lynn DeMaris
Editor: Nicholas L. Cerchio III
Copy Editor: Kathy Dove
Book Design and Layout: Bob Schwartz

Library of Congress Cataloging-in-Publication Data

DeMaris, Sheri-Lynn.
 Macro magic for kids and parents : taking the mystery out of macrobiotic cooking / by Sheri-Lynn DeMaris.
     p. cm.
 Includes index.
 ISBN 978-1892142450
 1. Macrobiotic diet--Recipes--Juvenile literature. I. Title.
 RM235.D46 2009
 641.5'63--dc22
                        2009036656

Printed and bound in the United States of America.

Cover Illustration: Irene Piovanelli

Table of Contents

Acknowledgments

When one has many unanswered questions and is open to receive life's blessings, opportunities will knock. Truly inspirational experiences and teachers will appear. I was fortunate to have many of both.

Michio and Aveline Kushi embraced me, as they did so many millions of people throughout the world, with loving arms. They graciously shared with me their inspirational teachings about food and the ways in which it affects the body, mind and spirit. I was thrilled to be invited to Becket, Massachusetts, to study and to live at the Kushi Institute for several summers. I listened for hours on end to their wealth of valuable information. My unanswered questions about how to develop true health were finally being addressed! In addition, I volunteered to work at their week-long summer conferences held each year in New England colleges.

While living in Philadelphia in the early 1980s, I was fortunate to meet and to study with many of the Kushis' students who were living in the Philadelphia area. Marilyn and Howard Waxman invited me to live in their home for four years to learn macrobiotic cooking for people of all ages. Stan and Geraldine Walker and Melanie and Denny Waxman also provided additional inspiration through their teachings and advanced training they offered in the day-to-day practice of macrobiotics.

Other truly inspirational teachers that I worked with through the years include Jeanne van den Heuvel, Luisa Baranda, David Briscoe, Tom Monte, Hiroshi Hayashi and Adelbert and Wieki Nelissen. Each of these teachers served as an inspirational piece of the puzzle, offering me support, ideas and cooking techniques.

I was fortunate also to meet gifted individuals who studied and practiced shiatsu massage, acupuncture, chiropractic care and Reike. These people helped me to improve my health and stamina and they offered me insights into how the physical body grows and changes with the aide of a new, healthy diet. I received Shiatsu massage, chiropractic care and acupuncture as well as teachings on developing a spiritual mind from Shizuko Yamamoto, Anthony Vincent, MD, Master Seok Seo Park, Hideo Izumoto and Saul Goodman.

There were others, too, such as Dirk Benedict, who inspired me with his tenacity of spirit and his clear message about integrating the practice of macrobiotics into our daily lives. Dirk offered me inspiration for my creative projects.

And, of course, many thanks go to those who provided me stability through all the searching—my family and friends, especially my mother, Roberta, who taste-tested more than one thousand of my new recipes. With her wondrous, creative mind she provided humor to carry me through the hurdles of new growth and discoveries.

Last but not least I would like to thank the four individuals without whom this book would not be possible: my publisher, Nick Cerchio, of Cedar Tree Books, for believing in me; Bob Schwartz for his beautiful design and creative ideas; Kathy Dove for her copyediting and writing suggestions; and Monica Giannobile, who helped me initiate the publishing process with her gifts of research and writing.

Sheri-Lynn DeMaris

Introduction

Macro Magic for Kids and Parents is the first in a series of Macro Magic books designed to teach people of all ages how to prepare beautiful, mouthwatering, healthy meals and snacks using only the freshest organic ingredients. In addition, the Macro Magic series will teach you how to recognize and to choose healthy foods.

Staying on a path of healthy eating is ever more difficult in our present-day society. The demands of work and our busy lifestyles permit us less and less time in the kitchen. What's more, we are pressured by the media from the time we are young to purchase poor-quality food or to ask our parents to purchase it for us. The Internet, television and magazines contain messages that tempt us from the path of good food choices into a thicket of ill health because the more unhealthy foods we choose to consume, the less our taste buds and bodies crave healthy foods and the more sickness we experience.

That is why I have designed the Macro Magic series for you. *Macro Magic for Kids*, the first book in the series, will be followed by other editions for meal preparations and healthy eating. *Macro Magic for People on the Go* will contain simple and quick recipes for the working adult; *Macro Magic for Singles* will present fun recipes for one; *Macro Magic for Moms* will contain more involved recipes for the family; *Macro Magic for Spas* will introduce an entirely new way of simplifying and lightening your cooking; and *Macro Magic for Seniors*, the last book in the series, will contain enjoyable time-saving cooking techniques for individuals who may be spending less time in the kitchen.

While working with people of all ages in hands-on cooking classes, I discovered that when individuals are given the opportunity to create healthy food dishes using the finest ingredients (and to grow them in the garden), they are much more likely to eat such ingredients on a regular basis and to repeat the cooking process at home. I also discovered that the longer people repeated this process, the more their taste buds changed and they actually began to crave nutritious foods. A simple way to change one's eating habits, don't you think!

I learned from working with people during my travels that the key to healing the body and maintaining long-term health lies in cooking with fresh, organic foods from the garden, complemented by ingredients from the macrobiotic standard diet: miso, which is used in a daily soup, helps to repair the intestines and to remove heavy metals from the body; shoyu, a naturally fermented soy sauce that aids digestion; umeboshi plums, which help to alkalize the blood and to keep the immune system strong; brown rice, which enhances the entire body by offering a continuous, even flow of blood sugar and fiber to the body; and sea vegetables, which add good quality minerals such as calcium and magnesium to the diet.

Surprisingly, these are some of the same foods recommended by the United States Department of Agriculture in its new food pyramid. Both sources emphasize the importance of using whole grains, beans, vegetables and fruits most often in the daily diet. Macrobiotics adds sea vegetables, naturally fermented soy products and vegetable pickles.

In my recipes I recommend using a number of ingredients, organic products and mild sweeteners that may not be familiar to all readers, so I have included Know Your Ingredient sidebars throughout the book to explain what each product is and what it looks like. These ingredients can be found in health food stores or in the health-food sections of many supermarkets. Those who do not live close to such markets can shop on Internet sites that carry natural food products.

When considering the costs of the finest organic products, remember that they will save you money in the long run. Doctor visits—and days missed from school or work—will be reduced; ear and throat infections, fevers, flues and colds will decrease and you will be less vulnerable to serious illness.

The books in the *Macro Magic* series will help you stock your kitchen—your true medicine cabinet. Once your kitchen cabinet is filled with these flavorful, wholesome ingredients and they become regular passengers in your shopping cart, you will find unhealthy snack attacks occurring less frequently or disappearing altogether; and as you begin to understand how to prepare healthy, macrobiotic foods, you will find it easier to pull out and dust off those old favorite recipes you have stored away and to re-work them using some of your own creativity. And as an added bonus, you will have more energy to do all of this!

Macro Magic cooking is designed to put you in touch with the natural cycles and processes of living. During our journey on Earth we need good quality air, water and food to live a full life. In addition, wholesome, well-balanced food preparation is a must for continued health on this planet. Create, cook and enjoy foods that come from nature. Remember, you are a part of it and you deserve the best!

From my cooking experience—and from witnessing myself and others heal from various unhealthy conditions as a result of dietary changes—I can assure you that the ingredients chosen for these books are the most healing foods available. Countless books and research studies bear witness to the tremendous healing benefits of eating whole grains, vegetables, sea vegetables, fruits and fermented soy products on a daily basis. I hope to share that joy and pleasure with you in the most creative way possible. Moreover, cooking with these ingredients can be so creative because of the endless combinations possible from mixing and matching food. The longer you eat organic, health-promoting foods, the more energized you will feel and the more creative you will become.

So enjoy!

Hey, Kids

I have found that a lifetime of good health is a lifetime of happiness. The magic wand for maintaining good health—aside from getting adequate exercise, fresh air and sunshine—is eating good quality organic food. By learning how to make good food choices you are given a gift for life. Just this one key will open up and change you forever. The teachings in this book will help rid you of illnesses now and in the future and put you on the path to a much greater quality of living.

After you begin to follow these simple cooking instructions and to eat healthy foods and snacks on a regular basis, you will find your overall health becoming much better. Our bodies naturally heal when given the proper tools. You will be amazed at how fast your body begins to change.

As you begin to eat healthier foods, you will find your skin naturally begins to heal from cuts and bruises more quickly. Colds, flus, weight gain, mood swings and infections will magically disappear—so much so that your doctor may recommend that you no longer need to depend on daily medication such as your inhaler on the athletic field, weekly allergy shots, or, for girls, pain medication for cramps.

You may find yourself throwing away your pimple cream because your skin will clear up automatically. You will sleep deeper at nighttime and wake up refreshed; you will feel increased energy throughout the day; and you will have a bright, positive outlook on life. You will get better grades easily in school simply because you will be able to read and to write better from a relaxed and focused frame of mind.

Overall your confidence and your appearance will improve. You will feel more attractive with a slim physique, clear complexion and shinier hair. In fact your entire life direction will change as both your mood and your outlook on life become more and more positive!

How can all this occur from eating healthier foods? Let me tell you the secret: food changes your blood, which affects your entire body—the health of your heart, liver, brain, lungs, stomach, digestive tract and your skin. Eating well will maintain healthy, strong blood so you can enjoy all of these benefits throughout your life.

The foundations of good nutrition are provided to us through the soil, sun and rain that contribute to the nutrients contained in plants; but we often consume food in highly processed forms that do not deliver its full, health-providing benefits. Worse yet, if we continue to eat highly processed foods, they can make us less healthy in the long run.

The wonderful news is that you can obtain maximum nutrients from eating whole grains, beans, vegetables, sea vegetables, fermented soy products and fruits—and this book will show you how! If you are afraid of trying new foods such as sea vegetables and fermented soy products, just give them a chance. You'll love them once you try them in recipes and become familiar with them. Like whole grains, beans and vegetables, they are healing to the body because they are chock full of protein, vitamins, minerals and plenty of fiber, as I will explain in detail in Chapter 1.

You will reap these benefits and more because building good blood helps to strengthen your immune system. I know from experience. Let me share with you the story of how this book started.

In the fall of 2006, I took a journey with a group of twenty-five eleven- to thirteen-year-old students when I created a healthy cooking club for fifth and sixth graders at Valley Forge Middle School in southeastern Pennsylvania. We met once a week in our family consumer science room that housed seven teaching kitchens. Each week we voted on a favorite recipe, then I purchased the ingredients for that recipe at the local Whole Foods market or harvested them from our school garden. Sometimes the dishes were entrees, sometimes desserts.

I began by introducing these students to the new food products and the wonderful health benefits they provide for the body. I then explained and demonstrated the seven, basic, food-preparation techniques: boiling, steaming, sautéing, deep-frying, baking, pickling and pressure cooking—the same techniques that you will learn in Chapter 3. Besides spending many hours in the vegetable garden, we went on a field trip to a local community-supported farm, where we learned how good-quality organic soil was created and how the weather affects the natural growth of plants.

In the kitchen, the students watched as I prepared a dish and shared the cutting techniques with them. Then they broke up into groups of five to six students and went to their various kitchens to prepare that dish. They prepared and cooked one dish for themselves and one for a student in our after-school homework program. Some of the students had previous cooking experience; some did not.

I taught the students how to balance food energetically to make it taste good by explaining the two dynamic opposite energies in foods—yin (expanding energy) and yang (contracting energy)—which I will explain in detail in chapter one. By learning these key concepts, students were able to adjust seasonings and cooking styles to make foods more flavorful and balanced.

I began to discover that learning the seven styles of cooking, the principles of balancing food dishes through yin and yang and then eating foods prepared using these techniques constituted a magical bag of tricks that allowed students to open up creatively and to improve their health. They all began to experience the same changes I had experienced when I first started cooking and eating macrobiotic foods: a craving for healthier foods, improved physical health and development of creativity in the kitchen.

First, their interest in eating healthy foods more regularly began to increase and they began asking their parents to purchase some of these same ingredients and to repeat these recipes at home. Second, they began reporting to me that their health was improving as well as their moods. Third, as they became more experienced with preparing wholesome food, their ability to create balance and health in their cooking without relying on recipes developed and they began to create some recipes on their own.

In this book, I will provide you with the magical bag of tricks that will allow you to begin walking your own path to health and happiness—transforming your body, mind and spirit through an openness to the creativity needed to develop healthy food dishes on your own. Get ready for a fun and exciting ride! I have included some of the students' favorite recipes to help you along the way.

macro magic for kids and Parents

Taking the mystery out of macrobiotic cooking

The Magic Begins:

Selecting the Most Nutritious Ingredients

Chapter 1

1. Choose foods closest to nature and in their whole state.

2. Choose foods that do not contain chemicals or added sugars.

3. Choose naturally fermented foods with healing properties.

In the Macro Magic series and in my televised cooking program, *Tea with Sheri* (www.teawithsheri. com), I use those foods recommended for most frequent use in the United States Department of Agriculture's new food pyramid and in Michio Kushi's *Standard Macrobiotic Diet* (Becket, MA: One Peaceful World Press. February 1996. Paperback, 64 pages). These foods include whole grains and whole-grain products, beans and bean products, vegetables, sea vegetables, fruits, seeds and nuts, fermented soy products, pickles and mild grain sweeteners. Throughout my teaching—and cooking for—people of all ages, I found the ingredients mentioned above to be the most balanced and healing for the body.

Grains are complex carbohydrates that release a constant flow of sugar into the bloodstream in a much more even manner than simple carbohydrates do. Therefore, whole grains—particularly in the form of brown rice—are a staple of a nutritious diet. They are considered high energy foods.

Civilizations all over the world have relied on grains as a dietary staple. In fact, in ancient times the word *meal* meant grain. A few examples of the uses of grains include brown rice in China and Japan; corn in North America and South America; barley and buckwheat in Europe; millet in North Africa and China, where it was considered a holy plant; teff in Ethiopia; oats in Ireland; quinoa and amaranth in South America; kamut in Egypt; and spelt in the Middle East.

In traditional ways of eating, grains are complemented by beans, vegetables and pickles. The central food item in the diet is grain; vegetables and beans are secondary foods; and pickles complement them all. These foods provide the best source of complex carbohydrates, vitamins and minerals for the body.

Why are these foods becoming the new recommended foods?

Food studies have provided information on the benefits of whole grains, vegetables and beans over animal foods, which contain large amounts of fats, while grains and vegetables contain a tiny amount. That is why people who center their diets on meat, fish, eggs and other dairy products suffer from constipation and a host of ailments such as cancer and heart disease—and why switching to a grain-bean-

and-vegetables diet tends to heal this condition over time. You can bet if your aunt or uncle tells you, he or she, has high cholesterol, it is the result of eating too much meat and dairy foods.

Now before we get all excited about choosing grains, let's find out what a whole grain actually is. Whole-grain products are cereal grains that contain bran, germ and endosperm. Bran, the outer layer of the kernel that protects the grain from oxidation, contains vitamins minerals and protein. Germ, the seed of the grain, contains vitamins and oil. Endosperm, located in the center of the grain, provides nutrition in the form of starch, though it also can contain oils and protein.

In contrast to refined grains, which retain only the endosperm, whole grains are full of vitality and energy and can generally be sprouted if placed in water. Processed grains—even cracked grain or flour products—generally do not carry this live energy and will rot when placed in water because their life vitality is missing.

What are these wonderful gems called whole grains? They are brown rice (which comes in short, medium, or long grain), millet, barley, whole oats, wheat (including kamut, wheat berries and spelt) and teff, quinoa and amaranth (which some people consider wild grasses).

So why haven't we heard much about them?

Following the two world wars, large cereal-producing companies began processing grains and refining them. In addition to making oatmeal and corn grits from cracked grain products—i.e., those that have been crushed or cut into smaller pieces—these corporate giants further processed grain into flour, baked it, added sugars to it, packaged it, popped a toy in the box and marketed the result as dry breakfast cereal that needed milk to re-hydrate it.

These companies then began to mill whole grain into flour, but instead of making hearty, whole wheat flour, they processed the grain further and took out the bran and sometimes bleached the grain to create white flour. These baked, sugary flour products—far removed from the nutritious grains they once were—became so popular that they now line the shelves of our supermarkets and convenience stores.

The exciting news is that you can choose to eat more whole grains daily—or at least cracked grain until you get up to speed. Just by adding a cracked grain or even rolled oatmeal to your breakfast menu, you can benefit from the soluble fiber that dissolves in water, makes oatmeal creamy and is known for its ability to control cholesterol levels.

After you read this book and learn how to cook whole grains, you can add insoluble fiber, which is found in brown rice and the other grains we have mentioned, to your diet. This fiber is excellent for cleaning the digestive tract and preventing all types of illnesses such as cancer and heart disease.

Bountiful Beans

Beans are an excellent source of protein, complex carbohydrate, vitamins and minerals, particularly calcium, thiamin and iron. Lower in fat than meat, beans are much easier to digest and they move through the intestines and the digestive system more quickly and with fewer toxins. High in phosphorus and vitamin E, beans—especially adzuki and soy beans—are a good source of iron.

Bean Products

These offer variety to the body but do not offer as much strength as the bean dishes. Bean products include tofu, tempeh and seitan.

Vegetables: Simple Gifts from the Garden

Fresh vegetables add a host of vitamins, minerals and cancer-preventing nutrients to your diet. Stock your refrigerator with the following vegetables, which you will use regularly: onions, carrots, cucumber, lettuces, collard greens, mustard greens, watercress, kale, cabbage, parsnip, burdock, parsley and scallions.

Some vegetables—tomatoes, white potatoes, eggplant, red and green bell peppers and hot peppers such as chili and paprika—should be limited because of their high acid content. As you progress, you may want to reduce or eliminate your intake of these vegetables because they have a higher acid content. These plants grow in the nighttime and their consumption can lead to arthritic conditions and other inflammations of the body.

Sea Vegetables: Gems from the Ocean

Although not so common in America, sea vegetables such as nori, which kids love to eat as a snack, wakame, kombu and hiziki—are used around the world. They contain abundant minerals and are easy to add to soups, salads and side dishes.

Less Concentrated Sweeteners

We use barley malt, rice syrup and, occasionally, maple syrup. Brown rice syrup and barley malt are the highest-quality sweeteners available. They are made by cooking rice and barley down to a thick, rich syrup. They can be substituted for sugar in any traditional recipe.

Brown rice syrup and barley malt provide a slow, prolonged source of energy in the body and a relaxing, calming effect on the mind. Because they are cooked down whole grains, they are metabolized more slowly in the body, thus producing less insulin. As a result, they tend to be less harmful for diabetics and they do not contribute as much as sugar does to tooth decay in children.

The students in our cooking classes used brown rice syrup and barley malt to sweeten sauces, soups and bean dishes. They also added these sweeteners to dips and spreads, just as you would with jams. We used maple syrup, which is less concentrated than other sweeteners on the market, to flavor our desserts.

Pickles, Seeds, Nuts and Beverages

Pickles: organic sauerkraut, dill cucumber pickles (use naturally fermented pickles).
Seeds: non-tropical seeds such as pumpkin, sesame and sunflower; nuts: almonds, cashews, walnuts, chestnuts and pecans.
Beverages: a variety of grain-based beverages such as bancha, twig tea and barley tea; the following have little traces of caffeine and help to relax the body: grain coffee, made from chicory and amasake, a fermented rice drink. Soy or rice milk should not be consumed on a daily basis, but they can be used to replace milk in some of the recipes.

More Than Enough Protein

Banish your fears of not getting enough nutrients from these new recommended foods. Whole cereal grains, beans and bean products, nuts and seeds and a variety of vegetables provide more than the needed amount of protein for our bodies. Miso and shoyu also contain essential amino acids.

A Rainbow of Vitamins

Vitamin A: found in green, leafy vegetables such as kale, mustard greens, collard greens, dandelion, etc. and carrots.

Vitamin B 1: sea vegetables, almonds, soybeans and their products, brown rice, lentils and other beans.

Vitamin B2: sunflower seeds, soybeans and their products, pinto beans, millet, wheat, rye, sesame seeds and lentils.

Vitamin B12: fermented foods such as miso paste, shoyu sauce, tempeh, natto and sea vegetables.

Vitamin C: green, leafy vegetables such as watercress, collard greens, carrot tops, etc. and cauliflower, cabbage and bancha twig tea.

Vitamin D: fresh vegetables, sunlight.

Vitamin E: brown rice and all whole cereal grains, nuts, beans and green leafy vegetables.

Vitamin F: sesame and olive oils.

Vitamin K: green, leafy vegetables such as cabbage, parsley, collard greens, etc. and brown rice; also produced in the intestinal flora.

An Abundance of Minerals

Calcium: Americans mistakenly believe that dairy food must supply their needed calcium, yet there is plenty of calcium in a plant-based diet; what's more, green leafy vegetables, sesame seeds, sea vegetables, nuts, sunflower seeds and tofu are the primary sources of calcium in many diets throughout the world.

Magnesium: sea vegetables, soybeans and their products, lentils and green leafy vegetables.

Phosphorus: whole grains, sea vegetables, nuts, beans and bancha twig tea.

Potassium: sea vegetables, soybeans and their products, dried fruits, nuts and vegetables such as kale, turnip, cabbage and cauliflower.

Iron: sea vegetables, sesame seeds, beans, brown rice and green vegetables such as parsley, kale, dandelion greens, etc. and cast iron cookware.

Iodine: sea vegetables and green leafy vegetables.

Sodium: sea vegetables, green leafy vegetables, dried fruits, celery, sea salt, miso and shoyu sauce.

The following foods also contain a small amount of fats and oils: whole grains, especially oats and all vegetables. People without serious health problems benefit from naturally occurring oils and can add a small amount of cooking oil if dairy foods are not part of their diets.

Extra Exciting Bonus—Antioxidants!

Vegetables and fruits are full of antioxidants—substances that protect plants from oxygen free radicals, dangerous oxygen molecules that can attack the body's chromosomes and cause cells to loose their basic function and to multiply out of control, creating cancers in the body. Antioxidants, including beta-carotene, lycopene, Vitamin E, selenium and Vitamin C, translate into special cancer-fighting properties that protect the body from free radicals.

Extra Extra Bonus—Phytochemicals!

Cruciferous vegetables (broccoli, cabbage and collard greens), which get their name from the crossed-shaped flowers that adorn them in the garden, are rich in phytochemicals, the natural chemicals found in plants. Phytochemicals change the way estrogen is broken down and eliminated in the body. Estrogen often builds up in the bodies of people eating an animal-based diet. Cooking is said to reduce phytochemicals. It does somewhat, but it doesn't eliminate them. Phytochemicals are also found in allium vegetables—onions, scallions, shallots, chives, garlic and leeks.

Added Bonus of Healing

The body will heal itself naturally when it is given the correct support and an environment in which to do so. Certain foods from the earth have a healing quality. That is why they are so important to include in our diets. Ancients knew the healing secrets of food and developed many food remedies for various illnesses. The signature of foods, revealed by their shape and texture, sometimes indicates what part of the body these foods help to heal.

Carrots, for example, help strengthen the intestines; lotus root strengthens the lungs; round vegetables strengthen the spleen, pancreas and stomach; and fast upward growing vegetables such as scallions help to lift the energy in the body.

How to Choose Foods

Vegetables and grains supply all the nutrients your body needs to grow and to stay balanced. Processed foods do not. Our bodies are made of decomposed foods. Everything you have ever eaten, including the food you ate in your mother's womb, has contributed to the formation of your organs, including your skin, hair and nails, your bones and nervous system. Do you really want junk food to play a part in forming these systems in your body?

Good blood is essential to good health. Red blood cells have a nucleus of iron. Iron is used to make compass needles because it is very sensitive to electric currents and is easily magnetized. When our cells are in good condition, they automatically point us toward the right direction, enabling us to enjoy the utmost flexibility and to adapt to any environment or change of circumstances while moving to our greatest goal—good nourishment. The only way to maintain our blood quality is through good eating because our blood cells are produced directly from what our bodies absorb through our small intestines.

The acid and alkaline contents of various foods are important in cooking. By selecting foods carefully, you can help your body do its job of balancing itself. The main objective is to keep your blood as alkaline as possible because too much acidity can create a tendency toward disease and other problems. If you eventually feel jumpy, unfocused and uncomfortable after eating a candy bar, your blood is becoming acidic.

In order to learn balanced cooking you must first learn the principles or the energy quality of food, then you must learn how to transform that energy through fire, salt and cooking time. Two pairs of opposites exist in nature: foods that are contracting and make us feel more tight and active; and foods that are more relaxing and help us to open up. The key is to balance these two in the healthiest way possible.

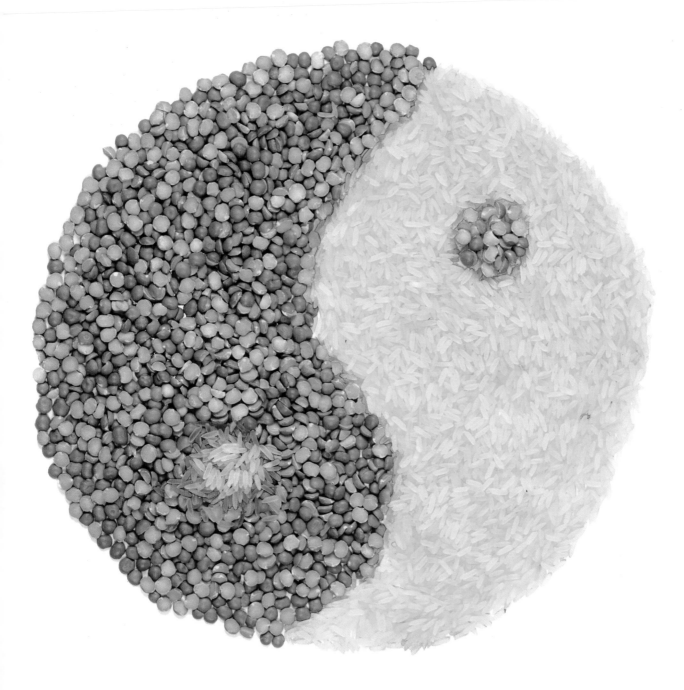

It is also helpful to eat according to the climate, your sex, body structure and age. Our bodies choose naturally to adapt to the environment. If we live in a warm climate, we naturally crave more tropical fruits and vegetables in their raw state. We also crave foods that are considered yin (expanding, relaxing, cooling) and we seek fewer long-cooked animal foods, stews, heavy grains and root vegetables.

People who live in a colder climate crave more fats and more animal foods, which are considered yang (contracting, energizing, warming). They naturally eat fewer raw salads and fruit.

The differences in sex and body constitution also call for different kinds of foods. Men tend to be more physically active and possessed of a larger amount of muscle weight; therefore, they need more yang foods in their diets. Women tend to be more soft and relaxed; therefore, they need more yin foods support them.

Whole grains, especially brown rice, are considered the most balanced in terms of yin and yang energy. Simply adding whole grains to our diet helps us to become more balanced in these energies.

Moreover, the consumption of whole grains begins to makes us more sensitive to food and more able to choose intuitively the foods our bodies need.

As we did when we were children, we can begin to develop our sensitivity and to make the correct food choices: selecting more plant-based yang foods such as heavy grains, fatty beans and root vegetables (or even fish if we are not vegetarian) when we need more warm, active energy in our bodies; and choosing more yin foods when we want to cool off, relax and open ourselves up. If we learn these opposites and use them in our cooking—serving a salty dish to balance a sweet one, for example—we will not only enjoy the taste of our dishes, but also feel satisfied and energized.

Only by eating a clean diet for some time will we develop this sensitivity, which has been blocked because of our modern way of life: importing and consuming tropical fruits and vegetables such as bananas, papaya, etc. in the winter and having access to large amounts of animal food in tropical climates. The key is to be in touch with how we feel and to prepare and to choose our foods wisely.

We often explain to our classes that people crave a sugary dessert after eating a full plate of well-cooked meat because the body is trying to maintain balance. The acid and alkaline contents of various foods are important in influencing our food choices. By selecting carefully, you can help your body do its job of balancing itself. The main objective is to keep your blood as alkaline as possible because too much acidity can cause a tendency toward disease and other problems.

Foods are classified according to their chemical components, water content, growing traits as plants, textures and other important characteristics. Nature produces various foods as we need to eat them. In hot weather, more green, leafy vegetables and cucumbers grow to keep us cool. In the fall, round vegetables such as squash and pumpkins are available to help warm the body by contracting it and reducing excess liquid built up during the summer months. In winter, root vegetables become available to strengthen our intestines and to further reduce liquid and acid in the bloodstream, thus keeping our bodies warm. Sea vegetables can be stored throughout the year and are appropriate for year-round use.

Learn the energies of yin and yang, but remember these are simply cognitive tools to help you get started. Once you understand them, begin to feel them. The more you eat well, the more it will happen automatically. It's not that much work. Just listen to the small voice inside the pit of your stomach when you take ingredients out of your cabinet. Listen to the message they provide you—one of happiness and relaxation or tightness and discomfort.

If we were to ask you to describe something in detail that you know well—a toy you wanted to buy, for example—and ask you to explain how you envisioned this toy you wanted before you actually went out and got it, you would be able to describe it in detail and to share the emotional feel or vibration it provided for you before it was manifested.

You should be able to do the same with food. You need to visualize the plate, feel and sense the taste and smell of food and how it will make you feel when you eat it. See it in your mind's eye. When you cook for others, see how they will interact with the foods you are preparing and envision how their bodies will change after they have eaten those foods.

Lastly, the most important ingredient in your cooking is your mental attitude! Bringing love to the kitchen is the most powerful healing mechanism. A close friend once reminded me of a Mahatma Gandho quote: "Be the Change you want to see in the world." After mulling this over for a long time, we came to the conclusion that Ghandi didn't mean to talk about change, nor to just philosophize or teach about change, but to implement and be the change.

We are born into this universe knowing that we have the capacity to envision and to desire anything we choose. Unfortunately, early in life, through conditioning and our upbringing, we are taught that we are not entitled to or capable of doing this. Even when we wallpaper our house with mantras and affirmations and tell our friends we are changing, nothing changes until we believe in what we want to change and follow through with concrete action.

Choosing to eat healthy food with love helps us with this process.

The Magical Wand:

Your Kitchen Equipment

Chapter 2

Setting up your kitchen, which is your real medicine cabinet, requires a lot of work. You may be familiar with some of the utensils you will need for macrobiotic cooking, but other items may not be familiar to you. To help you stock your medicine cabinet properly, I have included an entire list of the utensils you will need as a reference in this series of books.

Stove—gas or wood preferred over electric or microwave. Just as we choose the most healing foods, we select the most natural form of heat to cook our food. Wood stoves are ideal, but since many homes do not have them, gas stoves are the next closest form of natural heat to which people have access. Chefs choose gas over electric stoves or microwave ovens, which give food a dull, unsatisfying taste. A gas flame has more vitality and life energy and is easier to adjust. From my experience in cooking for various people with health concerns, their bodies tended to heal much more quickly with foods prepared on a fire.

Pressure cooker—stainless steel or enamel-coated for cooking rice and sometimes beans and chestnuts.

Frying pan with lid—cast iron or stainless steel for roasting nuts and seeds and for sautéing.

Cooking pots—stainless steel, cast iron, Pyrex®, stoneware, or enamelware are all good; aluminum or Teflon®-coated pots are not recommended because they are softer and toxic particles from the insides of these pots can leach into your meals.

Clay nabe pot with a lid—for steaming vegetables, grains and bean dishes.

Metal flame deflectors—help to distribute heat evenly and to prevent burning.

Suribachi—a ceramic grater with grated edges on the inside, used with a wooden pestle called a surikogi to purée and to mash seeds and condiments for dressings and sauces.

Metal or ceramic flat grater—to grate vegetables.

Pickle press—to press vegetables into a pressed salad or to pickle. A heavy bowl and a weight may be used in lieu of a pickle press.

Wooden cutting board—keep well oiled to prevent cracking; adjust to waist level to provide good leverage while cutting fruits and vegetables.

Vegetable-cutting knife—stainless steel, carbon steel, or porcelain.

Sharpening stone—for the knife.

Steamer insert—bamboo or stainless steel.

Long stainless steel blade fine mesh zester—for finely grating mochi.

Foley food mill—for puréeing soups and dressings.

Glass jars—large and small, to store grains, beans, seeds, teas and sea vegetables.

Glass refrigerator storing containers—with glass or plastic lids.

Shoyu dispenser—glass with plastic top.

Stove top tea pot and tea strainer—bamboo strainer is ideal.

Vegetable-scrubbing brush—with natural bristles to clean the outside skins of fruits and vegetables.

Wooden utensils—spoons, rice paddles, cooking chopsticks are suggested.

Bamboo mats—for covering cooked dishes and for rolling sushi.

Serving and mixing bowls—glass or ceramic.

Stainless steel strainer—fine mesh, for blanching and deep frying vegetables.

Small hand-held blender—used to blend dressings, soups and sauces; easier to use than a large blender or Quisinart®.

High-quality water filter —(or purchase spring water) because water and salt (see following item) are the two most important ingredients for our bodies.

Sea salt—choosing a good sea salt is extremely important because sea salt contains many beneficial minerals for our bodies that regular table salt does not.

True Alchemy:
Cook and Change the Energy of Food

Chapter 3

Cooking begins the process of breaking down food so that we can digest it more easily. When we cook, we control the discharge of nutrients from the center of food to its periphery in order to make those nutrients more available for the body to absorb through the intestines. We use a variety of cooking styles that produce an energetic impact on the body and begin the digestion process. Just as macrobiotic cooking considers the energy of foods in making food choices, it also considers the energy of various cooking methods and their effect on the body, taking into account the amount of flame used, cooking time and pressure. Salt, or salty seasoning, influences this process as well.

Cooking Styles

Pressure cooking—a method of cooking in a sealed pot that does not permit air or liquids to escape below a preset pressure; because the boiling point of water increases as the pressure increases, the pressure built up inside the cooker allows the liquid in the pot to rise to a higher temperature before boiling; pressure cooking is used primarily for grains and beans because it increases their digestibility; foods are cooked much faster by pressure cooking than by other methods, so dishes can be ready sooner.

Sautéing—creates movement in the food and activity in the dish, thereby creating more activity and circulation in your body when you eat sautéed foods; sautéing also tends to make dishes richer, especially those sautéed in oil, as the vegetables are cooked longer and release their water in a steady, long stream; finally, long sautés can enhance a protein dish and make it richer.

Steaming—is an upward, energetic way of cooking that helps steamed foods open and relax the upper body, including the lungs; it is, however, dehydrating, so it should not be used exclusively; heat rapidly disperses during steaming and this ultimately creates a cooling effect.

Baking—the most yang form of cooking, baking drives heat inside food while drying its outside, thus helping your circulation to carry that heat deep into the body and to give it warmth.

Boiling—lightens up the stomach area and brings out the brightness in the complexion by increasing the circulation in the face, giving it a more even glow.

Blanching—a method of food preparation in which food—usually a vegetable or a fruit—is plunged into boiling water, removed after a brief, timed interval, then submerged in iced water or placed under cold running water (shocked) to halt the cooking process; blanching loosens the skin on some fruits or nuts and enhances the flavor of some vegetables, such as broccoli, by releasing bitter acids stored in the food; blanching enhances the color of some (particularly green) vegetables by releasing gases trapped in the food that obscure the greenness of the chlorophyll; blanched foods are refreshing to the body.

Pressing/Pickling—a food-preservation method in which lightly salted vegetables are enclosed in a container and subjected to pressure, which, along with the salt, causes the juices to seep from the vegetable and form a mild brine that pickles the vegetable; pressing/pickling can last anywhere from three hours to three days; it ferments vegetables, allowing the creation of digestive enzymes that enhance the function of our digestive tracts; the energy of eating a pressed salad releases stored up pressure in our bodies, creating a relaxed feeling.

Long steaming (Nishime)—also called "waterless cooking," Nishime involves layering cut vegetables in a pot along with a tiny amount of water, covering the pot with a heavy lid, then heating it over a high flame until a very hot steam is produced inside; the flame is then reduced to as low as possible and the vegetables are cooked from 20 to 50 minutes, depending on the amount and kind of vegetables cooked. Nishime-style cooking makes vegetables strong-tasting and sweet, while driving salt deep inside them. Long steaming has the same effect on us when we eat long-seamed foods—it strengthens the core of the intestines, stomach and pancreas, giving us endurance.

Nabe cooking—used primarily to cook vegetables, nabe cooking (or slow simmering in a soft clay pot) makes vegetables soft and pliable and thus softens and relaxes our bodies.

How to Correct Cooking Mistakes

If you taste a dish toward the end of its preparation and you want to make adjustments to it, try the following:
- Too sweet, add a little shoyu or ume vinegar.
- Too bitter, add some brown rice syrup or barley malt.
- Too salty, add raw veggies, pasta, or raw tofu.
- Too sour, add more shoyu, ume vinegar, or sea salt.
- Too pungent (ginger taste), add more salt.

COOKING SHORT CUTS

Time Savers

➥ Cook a large batch of beans ahead of time and reuse in various dishes.

➥ Cut up strips of kombu and wakame and keep in jars, where they will last forever. Some amazing healing foods such as miso, shoyu (naturally fermented soy sauce), umeboshi vinegar, brown rice vinegar and umeboshi plums and paste do not ever need to be refrigerated.

➥ Roast seeds and nuts ahead of time and keep them in jars, where they will remain fresh for two to three weeks.

Short Cuts to Avoid

➥ Avoid freezing or canning as it reduces the energy and vitality in food.

➥ Fermenting is fine, however, as it pickles the food, which makes it more digestible.

Magic Potions:
*The Recipes

*Some recipes indicate certain amounts of spring water to be used, but the exact quantity may need to be adjusted, depending on the age of the grain/bean/vegetables, stove heat and climate. Check periodically during cooking and adjust water amounts accordingly, to prevent burning and to obtain the desired consistency.

Chapter 4

The recipes in *Macro Magic for Kids and Parents* range from healthful substitutes for junk food to traditional ethnic foods to basic macrobiotic dishes. These recipes have been divided into sections: soups, minicourses, main courses—including breakfast, lunch and dinner entrées—salads and desserts and drinks. Within each section you will find easy recipes as well as more difficult ones.

The best introduction to macrobiotic cooking begins with learning the recipes for short-grain organic brown rice, miso soup, basic salads and simple vegetable dishes. Eating these foods on a regular basis can improve your health quickly.

Through trial and error—and eventual success—you can familiarize yourself with magical, healing foods and the ways in which they work to promote good health. Before long you will be using your newly acquired knowledge to create appetizing, healthful meals. The combinations of grains, beans, bean products, vegetables, sea vegetables and fruits are endless.

Macrobiotic cooking takes into account the fact that our bodies are constantly making adjustments to the environment. Our cravings for certain foods often change in response to our activity level, the climate and our emotional state. When you enter the kitchen, think about your food cravings and your children's cravings and use that feedback as a basis for choosing a recipe. For example, when it's cold and damp outside, a long-cooked, salty, heavy dish will help to warm you up. In warm or hot weather a cool, refreshing, light dish will help cool you off.

Feel free to adjust the seasonings in these recipe to suit your own and your children's tastes and keep in mind the rule for salt: keep foods slightly sweeter tasting and less salty for children younger than ten years of age.

Kids delight in learning these recipes, which help them to acquire confidence in their ability to prepare good food—and the curiosity to try new items. If your children are young and would like to learn how to cook, invite them into the kitchen to cook with you. Make sure to supervise them carefully, especially when you are using knives and working near the stove.

Simmering Soups

Soup is a great introduction to any meal: it helps to relax the body and calm the mind, in addition to preparing the stomach for digesting the rest of the meal.

For cooking beginners, soup is one of the easiest dishes to prepare successfully. One can create an endless variety of soups utilizing different combinations of grain, pasta, vegetables and beans. Salty additions such as miso, shoyu, sea salt and umeboshi vinegar help to create soup with an alkalized base, which helps to aid in digestion.

By varying the ingredients, one can prepare a seasonal soup dish. Light broths with corn and quick-cooking greens help to brighten a soup for hot-weather consumption, while dense, heavy grains, beans and sea vegetables produce a stronger, warming dish for the winter months.

Kids love soups and recipes such as these help to provide them with plenty of nutrients.

Vegetable & Alphabet Soup

Yields: 5-6 cups

1 TBS extra virgin olive oil
1 onion, diced
Pinch of sea salt
¼ cup rutabaga, cubed
2 stalks celery, cubed
1 carrot, cubed
¼ cup corn (organic corn in season
or frozen organic corn)
¼ cup fresh shiitake mushrooms, sliced
1 pinch oregano
1 qt. spring water or vegetable broth
(left over from blanching vegetables)
1 bay leaf or a 1-inch piece of kombu
½ cup vegetable alphabet pasta
or any other shape children will enjoy
2 TBS shoyu

Heat olive oil in a large saucepan; add onion.

Sauté for 2-3 minutes or until transparent; add a pinch of sea salt.

Mix in rutabaga, celery, carrot, corn, mushrooms and oregano.

Sauté for another 3-4 minutes.

Add spring water (or vegetable broth) and then, bay leaf or kombu.

Simmer 3-5 minutes.

Add alphabet pasta.

Simmer 5 minutes until pasta is cooked thoroughly.

Season with shoyu.

Tip from the Chef

Vegetable broth can be substituted for spring water in all soup recipes. Vegetable broth is made by boiling fresh or leftover vegetables in spring water. Vegetable broth can be stored in a glass jar for up to three days.

KNOW YOUR INGREDIENTS - KOMBU

Kombu and bay leaves are used to flavor soup broths. Kombu adds minerals to the broth. When soaked and cooked with beans or vegetables, the broth helps soften and make them more digestible.

Creamy Corn Soup

Yields: 4-5 cups

1 tsp sesame oil
1 onion, diced
Pinch of sea salt
1 cup plus 1 TBS vegetable broth
or spring water
1/8 cup rolled oats
2 cups fresh or frozen corn (organic)
¼ tsp basil
¼ tsp oregano
¼ tsp thyme
¼ tsp sage
1 cup soy milk
2 stalks celery, cubed
black pepper to taste
2 TBS shoyu

Heat oil in a saucepan; add onion, a pinch of sea salt and 1 TBS of spring water.

Simmer until onion turns clear.

Cover onions with 1 cup of vegetable broth or spring water and bring to a boil.

Add oats, corn and spices.

Cook for 15-20 minutes until oats become soft.

Place in a blender with soymilk; blend until creamy.

Return to a saucepan and bring to simmer.

Add celery and cook until celery becomes bright green.

Season with pepper and shoyu.

Tip from the Chef

Oats and soymilk are used in this recipe to make a thick, creamy broth. Make sure to use original flavor soy milk without added cane sugar.

KNOW YOUR INGREDIENTS - ORGANIC CORN

Make sure to purchase organic corn in season or frozen organic corn. Non-organic vegetables may have been genetically engineered. For the same reason, always use organic products—garlic, onion, etc.—as much as possible.

Creamy Mushroom Soup

Yields: 4-5 cups

1 TBS sesame oil
2 cups of mushrooms, washed and sliced
1½ tsp dill
¼ tsp black pepper
1 cup soy milk
1 tsp lemon juice
1 TBS kuzu
3 TBS shoyu
½ cup spring water

Heat an iron skillet.

Brush skillet with sesame oil.

Add mushrooms, 1 TBS of shoyu and spices and cook until mushrooms are soft, about 5 minutes, then set aside.

Place soy milk, 1 TBS shoyu and lemon juice in a medium-size saucepan.

Dilute Kuzu in 1/2 cup spring water, then whisk kuzu into soymilk mixture and simmer until it turns from cloudy white to clear and the mixture thickens.

Add seasoned mushrooms and simmer 5 minutes longer.

Adjust taste with more shoyu if needed.

Tip from the Chef

Modify this recipe to create a thick sauce for noodles by adding 2 additional tablespoons of kuzu and 1 additional tablespoon of shoyu.

KNOW YOUR INGREDIENTS - KUZU

The kuzu (*Pueraria lobata*) plant has been used as a food in China for more than two thousand years—and praised in Japanese poetry and legend as a bracing health food and ideal thickener for more than a thousand years. Its roots are among the largest in the world, ranging in length from three to seven feet and weighing between 200 to over 400 pounds. Kuzu is used as cornstarch is, but kuzu is much more healing to the body. Kuzu must always be dissolved in a cold liquid first and gradually heated up. Otherwise lumps will develop and the liquid will not thicken.

Miso Soup

Yields: 3-4 cups

5 cups vegetable broth or spring water
1-inch piece wakame sea vegetable
1 dried shiitake mushroom
soaked in spring water and finely chopped

1/8 cup firm tofu, cut into ¼-inch cubes

To create a truly balanced miso soup, add one root, one round, and one green, leafy vegetable.

Here are some suggestions:
¼ finely sliced root veggie
(burdock, carrot, daikon, lotus root, or parsnip)

¼ cup finely sliced round veggie
(cabbage, rutabaga, turnip, or onion)

¼ cup finely sliced greens
(collard, kale, watercress, mustard greens, and/or turnip greens)

2 tsp Barley miso

Make broth by putting water into a saucepan with wakame sea vegetable.

Bring to a boil, (if using onion, add chopped onion and simmer until clear).

Add the remaining ingredients except for the greens, simmer until soft.

Add greens at the end of cooking and simmer until bright in color.

Transfer about 1 cup of broth from the pot into a measuring cup and add 2 teaspoons of barley miso.

Stir with a spoon until completely dissolved, then return mixture to pot and bring to a low simmer for 2-3 minutes.

Bring to a low simmer for 2-3 minutes until clouds form on top (do not boil as it will destroy enzymes in the miso.

Garnish with finely chopped parsley, scallion, chives, or grated ginger and serve warm.

Tip from the Chef

Keep your miso soup mild in taste especially for children, who are small and active and should not be given too many foods with a salty taste. If you make miso too strong for people of any age, too many hunger and sweet cravings will occur.

KNOW YOUR INGREDIENTS - MISO

Miso is a wonderful food for people of all ages especially those working on restoring their health. The blend of simple ingredients

in miso provides many essential nutrients and health benefits. Miso is rich in antioxidants and protective fatty acids and it provides a healthy dose of Vitamin E. Miso boasts protein and Vitamin B12 and provides the minerals necessary to help boost the immune system. Much of miso's magic is attributed to fermented soy paste, which is used to make miso.

Creamy Carrot Soup

Yields: 3-4 cups

5 fresh carrots
2 onions, sliced thin
1 TBS olive oil
1 cup spring water
2 TBS white miso,
dissolved into ¼ cup spring water
½ tsp juice from a freshly grated ginger root
1 TBS parsley or scallions, chopped fine

Wash the carrots, cut into chunks, set aside.

Heat a large 4-quart soup pot and add olive oil.

Add onions and stir fry with the lid off until lightly brown.

Add carrots and water, cover and cook for ½ hour.

When carrots become soft, turn off the heat and place the cooked vegetables into a blender.

Blend until soft and creamy; add more water if needed to create a soupy consistency.

Place mixture back into the soup pot and season with white miso and ginger.

Serve warm in individual bowls and garnish with Cilantro Tofu Sour Cream.

Cilantro Tofu Sour Cream

Yields: ½ cup

1/2 cup silken tofu
1/2 umeboshi plum
1 TBS cilantro chopped fine

Place ingredients in a bowl, blend with a hand blender.

Tip from the Chef

Parsnips, rutabaga, winter buttercup, haikado, or butternut squash can be substituted for the carrot to create a nice, sweet, creamy taste. Vary the amount of water in this recipe to create the thickness you desire

KNOW YOUR INGREDIENTS - WHITE & YELLOW MISO

Organic mellow white or yellow miso made from soybeans and rice koji works best in this recipe. Either one blends well with the sweet vegetables and adds a more delicate, sweeter taste and lightness to the soup than traditional brown miso does.

Japanese Noodles & Broth

Yields: 3-4 servings

½-pound package udon or soba noodles
3 quarts spring water

Garnish
2 red or white round radishes cut into thin slices
Nori strips or 1 square sheet of toasted nori
cut into quarters

Fill a 4-quart cooking pot with spring water and bring to a boil over a high heat, then add noodles, lower heat to medium and cook for 10 minutes.

Rinse and drain noodles, set aside.

Make Dashi Broth.

Place noodles in individual serving bowls and pour Dashi Broth over noodles, then garnish with toasted nori and radish slices and serve.

Dashi Broth
Yields: 4½ cup

4½ cups spring water
2 dried shiitake mushrooms

1-inch piece kombu
2 TBS shoyu

Soak mushrooms in ½ cup spring water for roughly 20 minutes to soften them, then remove from water and slice. Save soaking water and set aside.

Put 4 cups of spring water and a piece of kombu in a sauce pan, then add the shiitake mushrooms and their soaking water.

Cover and bring to a boil, then lower heat and simmer for 10 minutes and season with shoyu to taste.

Tip from the Chef

Many additional ingredients can be added to the broth: tofu cubes, slices of any root, round or green leafy vegetable such as carrot, lotus root, diakon, burdock, parsnip, Chinese cabbage, onion, watercress, collards and kale.

KNOW YOUR INGREDIENTS - JAPANESE NOODLES

Udon is a thick, wheat-flour noodle, which was brought back to Japan by Buddhist priests who had traveled to China to study Buddhism between the ninth and thirteenth centuries. Udon is usually served hot in a mildly flavored broth with various toppings. Dark brown broth, made from dark shoyu, is popular in eastern Japan, while light brown broth, made from light shoyu, is used in western Japan.

Soba is a thin Japanese noodle made from buckwheat flour. It is served chilled with a dipping sauce or in hot broth as a noodle soup. Soba is made from freshly harvested buckwheat and is known as "shin-soba." It also has more flavor and sweetness than regular soba.

Italian Bean & Vegetable Soup

Yields: 5-6 cups

1 tsp olive oil
1 onion, chopped fine
1 clove garlic, minced
1 8-ounce pack white mushrooms, sliced
¼ cup frozen peas
1 stalk celery, diced into ½-inch cubes
2 carrots, sliced rounds
½ tsp sea salt
¼ tsp pepper
2 cups tomatoes, chopped
1 15.5-ounce can canelli beans, drained and rinsed (or freshly cooked beans)
¼ cup finely grated mochi
2 TBS Italian parsley, separate into small leaves
2 TBS shoyu
5 cups water

Heat oil in a large saucepan.

Add garlic and onion.

Sauté with the lid off until the onions are clear and soft, about 3-4 minutes.

Add ¼ cup water, mushrooms, peas, celery and carrots.

Cook for 2-3 minutes.

Stir in tomatoes and beans.

Simmer covered for 20 minutes.
(You may add cooked pasta as well).

Season with shoyu, salt and pepper to taste.

Garnish with parsley and grated mochi.

Tip from the Chef

If a recipe contains onions, cook them first with the lid off the pan; this cooking method releases the acidic taste of onions and aides in digestion.

KNOW YOUR INGREDIENTS - CANELLI BEANS

Though any kind of bean can be used in this recipe, canelli beans are a fattier bean and add rich flavor to this soup. To use freshly cooked canelli beans in this recipe: soak dry beans overnight in one cup of spring water with a one-inch piece of kombu. Bring to a boil in a sauce pan, cover and cook for 1 hour or pressure cook for 45 minutes. Season with sea salt and simmer for 5 minutes. (Beans, in general, need to be cooked with salt at the end to help with digestion).

Millet Squash Corn Soup

Yields: 5-6 cups

1 cup millet
6 cups spring water
¼ cup chopped onions
¼ cup hard winter squash such as butternut, buttercup or Hokkaido pumpkin
¼ cup corn
¼ cup chopped celery
1 TBS white miso, diluted in ¼ cup spring water

Wash millet and dry roast over medium-high heat in a cast iron fry pan until golden brown.

Set aside and cool.

Bring water to boil in a saucepan.

Add onions, reduce heat and simmer with the lid off until clear.

Add squash, corn and millet.

Cover and simmer for 35-40 minutes until millet becomes creamy.

Add celery and miso.

Cover and cook 5 minutes until celery is bright green.

Tip from the Chef

When cooking grains in soups, it is best to add some sweet-tasting vegetables. Otherwise the soup will have a bland, flat taste.

KNOW YOUR INGREDIENTS - MILLET

Because millet is gluten-free, it is a good wheat substitute for those who suffer from Celiac disease or from the occasional bout of gluten sensitivity. Millet is a good source of magnesium and manganese. Research indicates that magnesium may reduce the risk of heart attack and phosphorus is important for the development of body tissue and energy metabolism.

Split Pea Soup with Croutons

Yields: 8-10 cups

2 cups split peas
6 cups spring water
1 bay leaf
1 cup onion, finely diced
2 carrots, diced
½ cup rutabaga, diced
2 stalks celery, diced
1 TBS shoyu
sprig of parsley to garnish

Rinse split peas in a strainer, then place in large sauce pan and bring to boil in 6 cups of spring water.

Skim off any foam that may develop on top of liquid.

Add bay leaf and onion, simmer for 10 minutes.

Add remaining vegetables and simmer for 30-40 minutes until peas are creamy and soft.

Add water as needed to reach desired creaminess.

Once peas are soft and creamy, add shoyu to taste.

Pour into individual bowls, add some croutons, garnish with parsley and serve.

Tip from the Chef

Split peas should be well cooked in order to dissolve them and to create a creamy consistency for the soup.

Croutons

**Yields: enough croutons for this recipe
and a sandwich bag full to store for your next soup meal**

8 slices whole wheat bread
4 cloves garlic, finely minced
(or use a garlic press)

2 TBS rosemary, finely minced
½ - ¾ cup olive oil

Mix garlic, olive oil and rosemary and set aside.
Cut bread into small pieces or into various shapes using small cookie cutters; then coat bread pieces with the garlic-olive-oil-rosemary mixture.
Heat an iron skillet on top of the stove over low heat and coat bottom with olive oil, then fry croutons on each side until brown and crispy.

KNOW YOUR INGREDIENTS - ROSEMARY

Rosemary adds a nice touch to croutons, baked vegetables and fried sweet potatoes. You can purchase it already dried or harvest some from the garden and dry it yourself.

Mystical Minicourses

Minicourses include finger-licking foods that kids love to snack on any time of day. Parents love minicourses too because they contain ingredients that help to build strong, healthy bodies. Some of these recipes can be prepared as appetizers and served before the main meal, or they can be used as a simple meal unto themselves.

Sushi

Yields: 4 rolls

4 sheets of toasted nori seaweed
1 cup of organic, short-grain brown rice
1½ cups of spring water
3 pinches of sea salt
2 TBS pickled ginger
(purchase a package of naturally pickled ginger with
shiso leaves and serve right from the package)

2 tsp wasabi
(use fresh wasabi or an all-natural version
that comes in powder form and can be reconstituted
by adding a small amount of spring water

Rice-Vinegar Seasoning
¼ cup of brown rice vinegar
¼ tsp of sea salt

Dipping Sauce

Use simple shoyu sauce or mix together any of the following with shoyu: brown rice vinegar, mustard, green tea, mirin, grated daikon, or wasabi.

Prepare Rice-Vinegar Seasoning*
Simmer ingredients in a saucepan until salt dissolves (approximately 7-10 minutes on low heat).

Place in a small bowl and allow to cool.

*Rice vinegar seasoning can be prepared the day before to enhance its taste.

Prepare Brown Rice
Place brown rice, water and sea salt in a pressure cooker or saucepan.

Pressure cook (or boil in a saucepan) for 45 minutes (see page 46).

Allow pressure to come down naturally if pressure-cooking.

Remove rice and place in a bowl to cool before adding seasoning.

Season Rice
Use 1/8 cup of the rice-vinegar seasoning mixture per cup of rice. (Leave the rest in the small bowl to use for keeping fingers moist while rolling).

Gently sprinkle seasoning over rice and stir in with a spoon (no need to put in a flat pan).

(continued)

SUGGETIONS FOR SUSHI FILLINGS

Mix and Match
Use about 2 tablespoons of ingredients for each roll. When choosing fillings, think about flavors such as sweet and salty that complement each other and imagine what colors look appetizing together.

Fun combinations kids have created!
Peanut butter and sauerkraut; almond butter and pickled ginger; blanched scallions; carrots and burdock with umeboshi paste.

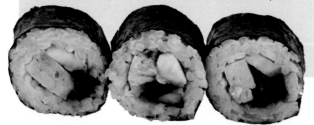

Other ingredients to mix and match
Fresh vegetables lightly blanched (carrots, asparagus, broccoli); marinated vegetables (pickles, radish, cucumber, rutabaga and gourd strips); fresh vegetables (avocado, cucumber, watercress); tofu (marinated in shoyu and water for 5 minutes or deep fried in safflower oil and then boiled in shoyu and water); tofu cheese (frost one 20-oz block of tofu with white or dark miso; allow to sit overnight covered with a cheesecloth; rinse tofu and cut into slices); shiitake mushrooms (prepared from dried state—soak in water for 5 minutes and simmer with shoyu and water for 7-10 minutes); sesame seeds (dry roasted in a pan); roasted tahini (sesame butter); mustard; wasabi.

Prepare Sushi Rolls

Lay out a clean bamboo mat.

Cover mat with one sheet of nori, shiny side up.

Press one handful of cooked rice on nori leaving one inch uncovered at the bottom and 1½ inches on top.

Make sure to wet hands and press the rice down firmly.

Make a groove in the rice near the center and arrange fillings.

Moisten edges of the nori with fingers dipped in vinegar-water and begin rolling, making sure to keep the sushi mat on the outside of the roll! Roll tightly.

Remove sushi mat and place roll, seam side down, until ready to cut.

Moisten knife; slice roll carefully into eight or more equal pieces.

Rinse knife between cuts.

Place a small amount of wasabi and pickled ginger on a plate.

Garnish with greens, vegetables, or flowers.

Fill small dishes with shoyu or shoyu mixture for dipping.

Tip from the Chef

Keep hands moderately moist at all times and press rice firmly onto the nori before rolling. Use one handful of rice and 2 TBS of filling for each roll. Do not attempt to add more. Otherwise, while you are rolling the sushi roll, excess rice and filling will fall out of the sides and go to waste. In addition the roll will not be firm enough to cut into attractive pieces.

KNOW YOUR INGREDIENTS - BROWN RICE VINEGAR

Brown rice vinegar is naturally brewed following a thousand-year-old recipe: brown rice, koji (a mold used for fermentation) and spring water are blended in clay crocks and aged underground for 6 - 12 months. The resulting vinegar is very mild, slightly sweet in flavor and less acidic than regular vinegars. Brown rice vinegar is used to make vegetable pickles that stimulate digestion and is a traditional seasoning for sushi.

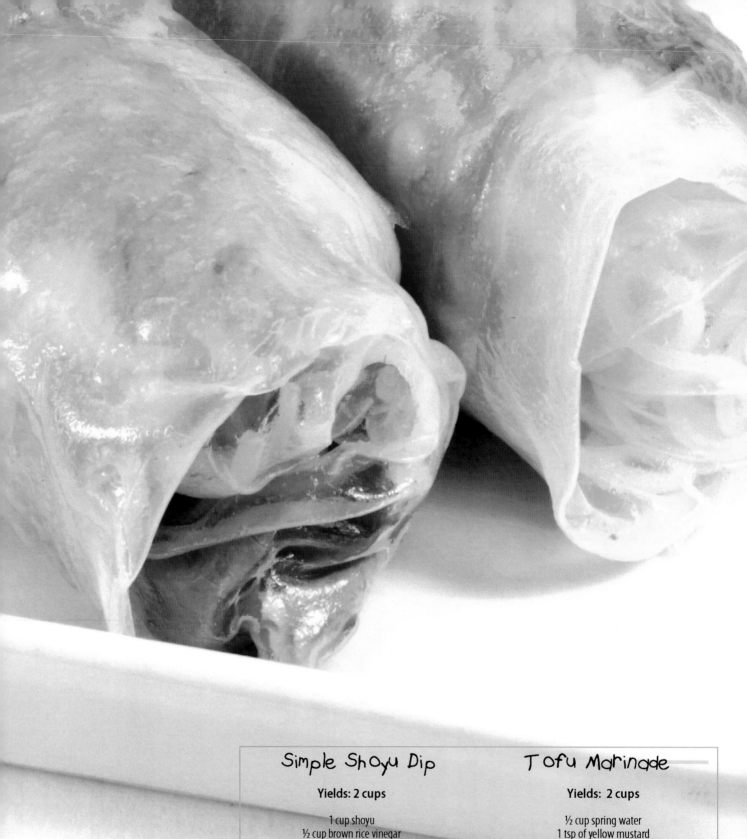

Simple Shoyu Dip

Yields: 2 cups

1 cup shoyu
½ cup brown rice vinegar
½ cup spring water
2 tsp toasted sesame oil
1 tsp sesame seeds, roasted
1/8 tsp fresh ginger juice

Mix all ingredients together and serve with the rolls.

Tofu Marinade

Yields: 2 cups

½ cup spring water
1 tsp of yellow mustard
1 tsp of shoyu sauce

In a bowl or deep dish combine spring water, yellow mustard and shoyu sauce.
Add tofu and marinate for 30 minutes.

Cold Vegetarian Spring Rolls

Yields: 8 rolls

1 cup carrot, cut into thin matchsticks*
1 cup mung bean sprouts, rinsed
1 cup Chinese cabbage, sliced thin
1 cup lettuce, sliced thin
½ cup red radish, sliced thin
½ cup cilantro, chopped fine
1 cup fresh, organic tofu, sliced thin
1 bunch of scallions, sliced thin lengthwise
8-9 inch round rice paper sheets, soaked in warm water for 45 seconds
4 cups spring water, placed in a shallow bowl
1 TBS sea salt

*Be creative and use other vegetables such as cucumber, zucchini, jicama, mushrooms, or daikon

Place cut vegetables together in a bowl.

Mix in sea salt until water comes out of the vegetables.

Press vegetable mixture by covering it with a plate and placing a heavy object on top of the plate to help reduce liquid.

Press for 6-10 minutes to remove any excess water.

Soak a rice paper sheet in a shallow bowl of spring water for 1-2 minutes, then lay the sheet on a cutting board.

Layer 2 TBS of the salad mixture and a few slices of the marinated tofu across the rice paper sheet.

Roll rice paper horizontally over the salad mixture as you would a sushi roll (see page 35), tucking one end in tightly.

Fold the left and right sides of the wrapper in and then continue to roll. This will give the roll the shape of an egg roll.

Seal end of the rice paper with a little water to make the sheet stick.

Tip from the Chef

Children enjoy helping to prepare this dish. They especially enjoy learning how to soak the wrappers and wrap the vegetables. Cold vegetarian spring rolls are cool and refreshing to the body, a wonderful dish to serve during hot summer months.

KNOW YOUR INGREDIENTS - TOFU

Tofu, which originated in ancient China, reached Japan during the Nara period (710 to 794 C.E.). Tofu is created by pressing soybeans for their milk and then fermenting that milk with a natural salt, *nigari*, so it coagulates into curds. Low in calories, tofu contains a relatively large amount of iron and little fat.
Because it has little flavor or smell of its own, tofu can be used in savory or sweet dishes.

Choose only organic brands of tofu because that not labeled organic may have been made from genetically engineered soybeans. Tofu should always be cooked or pickled with miso before eating because it (tofu) is a very yin (acidic) and cooling food. Otherwise it is extremely hard to digest. Only during very hot weather is tofu served raw and even then it is usually served with some grated ginger root and shoyu to aid in digestion.

Quick Mock Duck Sauce

Yields: 1 cup

¼ cup of brown rice syrup

¼ cup brown rice vinegar

4 TBS shoyu

1 tsp of juice from grated ginger root

juice and zest from one orange

1 TBS of kuzu,

dissolved in ¼ cup cold spring water

Place kuzu and spring water in a sauce pan. Cook over low heat until thick, stirring constantly.

Add rest of the ingredients.

Place in a small serving bowl and serve hot as a dipping sauce for the spring rolls.

Spring Rolls with Mock Duck Sauce

Yields: 10-12 rolls

1 TBS dark sesame oil, for stir frying filling
½ cup carrots, sliced into thin matchsticks
½ head of green cabbage, shredded fine
8 button mushrooms, sliced thin
¼ cup bean sprouts
½ cup firm tofu cut into thin slices
1 TBS shoyu
1 tsp juice from grated ginger root
2 TBS cilantro, minced
Store-bought spring roll wrappers
6 TBS light sesame oil, for frying rolls

Heat frying pan and add dark sesame oil.

Add carrots, cabbage and mushrooms and sauté for 3-4 minutes.

Add bean sprouts, tofu and shoyu. Sauté for 3-4 more minutes.

Season with ginger juice, then turn off heat and fold in cilantro.

Place square eggroll wrappers on a cutting board with one square edge facing the edge of the board.

Place 1-2 tablespoons of filling horizontally in the middle of the wrapper.

Fold bottom edge over the filling and side edges over the bottom edge (similar to folding the 3 sides of an envelope).

Roll and seal the top flap with cold water.

Heat frying pan and add light sesame oil to one-inch depth.

When oil is hot, place rolls in frying pan.

Cook until golden brown, rolling gently with a wooden spoon.

Remove, then drain excess oil from rolls on a brown paper bag and serve.

Tip from the Chef

Adding brown rice syrup and brown rice vinegar to shoyu creates a sweet and sour flavor often used in Chinese dips and sauces. This complements the taste of egg rolls nicely.

Replace sesame oil and seeds in dipping sauce with 1 tablespoon of nut butter for a richer taste.

KNOW YOUR INGREDIENTS - CILANTRO

Cilantro is the leaf of the young coriander plant, *Coriandrum sativum*, an herb in the parsley family, similar to anise. Coriander was cultivated in ancient Egypt and was used as a spice in both Greek and Roman cultures.

The early physicians, including Hippocrates, used coriander for its medicinal properties, including as an aromatic stimulant. The unique flavor of cilantro adds to the taste of spring rolls, fried egg rolls and wontons.

Tempura

Yields: 8-10 servings

¾ cup whole wheat pastry flour
1 TBS corn meal
1 TBS brown rice flour
1 tsp sea salt
1 cup cold nonalcoholic beer
½ cup broccoli, cut into flowerets
½ haikaido or buttercup squash,
seeds removed and cut into thin slices
2 sheets of nori, cut into one-inch squares
2 cups safflower oil

Dipping Sauce

½ cup spring water
2 TBS shoyu
1 tsp juice from grated ginger
1 tsp daikon, grated

Tip from the Chef

Tempura batter must be thick enough to cover the vegetables but not so thick as to become pasty and heavy when fried. If the batter sits too long before using, it will become too heavy and thick. Add more beer to thin it out. Keeping the batter very cold before coating the vegetables and placing them in the hot oil will make this dish very crispy.

Prepare the Dipping Sauce
Mix all ingredients together in a dipping bowl.

Prepare the Tempura Batter
Mix dry ingredients thoroughly in a bowl.

Add cold, nonalcoholic beer and stir gently with a chopstick.

Place in the freezer to keep chilled.

Fry the Tempura Batter Coated Vegetables
Heat safflower oil in a large, deep, cast-iron pan or heavy saucepan over medium heat.

Add a drop of batter to the oil.

- If the batter falls to the bottom of the pan, then rises and bubbles to the top, the oil is ready for deep-frying.
- If the batter stays on the bottom of the pan, the oil is too cool.
- If the batter doesn't fall but bubbles briskly on top of the oil, the oil is too hot.
- Adjust the heat if necessary.

Coat each vegetable lightly with batter, then drop into the hot oil.

Turn vegetables as needed to brown all sides of the tempura batter.

Remove vegetables and drain off excess oil by placing them on a metal rack or a brown paper bag.

Repeat the tempura process with the nori squares.

Arrange pieces nicely on a serving plate with the bowl of dipping sauce.

KNOW YOUR INGREDIENTS - GINGER

Pungent in flavor, fresh ginger root is often eaten with high protein or fatty foods in order to help with the digestion process. Ginger can be sliced into small pieces and added to soups and stews; it can be grated fine for use as a garnish; or it can be grated very fine and squeezed to yield a juice.

Mochi Sweet Rice & Chestnuts

Yields: 8-10 servings

½ cup of dried chestnuts
2½ cups of spring water
2 cups of sweet brown rice
three pinches of sea salt
¼ cup of organic apple juice
4 TBS light sesame seeds, roasted

Soak the chestnuts in ½ cup of spring water in a bowl overnight.

Place sweet rice in a pressure cooker with water and sea salt, then cover and cook for 45 minutes.

Remove cover and pound rice with a heavy wooden mallet until the kernels of rice become mushy and sticky. Set aside.

Remove chestnuts from spring water. Place them and apple juice in a pressure cooker. Bring to pressure and cook for 40 minutes.

Set aside to cool.

Wet hands and roll sweet brown rice into 1-inch balls. Place a cooked chestnut inside each ball and cover completely with the sweet rice.

Roll balls in roasted sesame seeds and place individually on a serving dish.

Tip from the Chef

Keep the wooden mallet wet while pounding the sweet rice and keep hands wet while rolling the rice, otherwise it will all end up as a sticky mess!

KNOW YOUR INGREDIENTS - MOCHI

Mochi (pounded sweet rice) can be handmade or purchased in a cake form already pounded. Its glutinous, sticky-sweet taste makes it a favorite among children. Instead of forming homemade mochi into balls, pound it further until the rice kernels are dissolved completely. Spread into a baking dish dusted lightly on top with brown rice flour; set aside to dry out overnight. Cut into squares, which can be pan fried, deep fried, or baked for a delicious treat!

Marinated Fried Tofu

Yields: 4-6 servings

1 package of tofu (20 ounces), cut in ½ inch slices
¼ cup whole wheat pastry flour
1 tsp black sesame seed
1 TBS sesame oil

Marinade
1 clove of garlic, crushed
1 tsp of shichimi (Chinese hot pepper)
2 small shallots, chopped fine
4 tsp mirin
½ cup shoyu

Dipping Sauce
1/8 cup shoyu
1 tsp grated fresh ginger
1 tsp grated fresh daikon

Place the marinade ingredients into a large shallow dish and mix well.

Add the tofu slices to the marinade, cover and leave at room temperature for 30 minutes.

Turn the slices over and marinate another 30 minutes on the other side.

In another bowl mix all the dipping sauce ingredients together.

Cover and set aside.

Remove the tofu slices from the marinade and dip in the flour mixture, then sprinkle with the black sesame seeds.

Coat the bottom of a medium-size frying pan with sesame seed oil.

Heat the oil, then fry the tofu slices in batches for 3 minutes on each side.

Drain and serve with dipping sauce.

Tip from the Chef

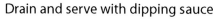

Grating the daikon and the ginger root with a very fine porcelain grater makes the dipping sauce blend nicely.

KNOW YOUR INGREDIENTS - DAIKON

Daikon is a large white radish that has a pungent flavor and helps to break down fat in the body. It is often used in dipping sauces used with tempura and other fried food recipes to help break down the oil and make the dish more digestible.

Tofu Nut Balls

Yields: 8-10 servings

½ cup uncooked short-grain brown rice
1 cup spring water
2 TBS shoyu
½ lb firm tofu, mashed
½ cup (rounded measure) ground almonds
½ cup whole wheat bread crumbs
sea salt to taste
1-2 TBS sesame oil
1 cup safflower oil
(optional, for deep frying)

Place the rice and spring water in a small saucepan. Bring to a boil, cover and lower the heat to the lowest possible simmer.

Cook until rice is very soft (mushy even), about 35-45 minutes.

Place the shoyu and half the mashed tofu in a blender or food processor and add about 3/4 of the cooked rice, then blend into a thick paste.

Place the remaining tofu in a medium-size bowl. Add the blended mixture, along with the almonds, bread crumbs and remaining rice. Add salt to taste.

Using your hands, form the batter into 1-inch balls (or if you have a heart-shaped cookie cutter, oil the cutter and press the batter into heart shapes).

Pan fry nut balls in 2 TBS sesame oil for about 15 minutes, bake them on a tray lightly oiled with 1 TBS sesame oil for about 30 minutes in an oven that's been preheated to 350°, or deep fry them in 1 cup of heated safflower oil. Serve hot.

Tip from the Chef

Tofu nut balls can be served as an appetizer, a snack, or on top of spaghetti in place of meatballs. Kids enjoy their roasted, nutty flavor.

KNOW YOUR INGREDIENTS - BREAD CRUMBS

Using Italian-flavored bread crumbs add a little more flavor to this dish. When shopping for bread  crumbs, select whole wheat bread crumbs with no added ingredients except spices.

Cucumber Bites

Yields: 10 servings

1 lb organic, extra-firm tofu, drained
1 TBS of white miso
1 tsp sesame butter
3 cucumbers, sliced into ¼-inch rounds

Place all ingredients except the cucumbers into a blender.

Blend until creamy.

Arrange cucumber slices on a serving plate.

Place a spoonful of blended tofu mixture on top of each cucumber round.

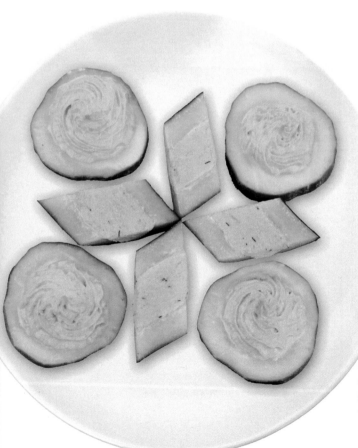

Tip from the Chef

The tofu mixture can be prepared a few days ahead of time. The white miso will ferment the tofu and give it a cheeselike taste. Thin the tofu blend with water to create a dip or dressing, or use it as a spread on bread or vegetables.

KNOW YOUR INGREDIENTS - UNWAXED CUCUMBER

Vegetable skins help to nourish our skin. When purchasing cucumbers, look for those that have not been waxed, so you can serve them with the skin on.

Magical Main Courses

Main courses are the heart of any meal, be it breakfast, lunch or dinner and with the exception of breakfast, usually rounded out with a side dish or two.

The recipes in this section cover the gamut from dawn to dusk with healthy, nutritious ideas for breakfasts that are high in the energy content needed to get the day off to a good start; creative lunches with some traditional favorites kids love, like tacos, burgers and pizza; dinners such as lasagna and stews that are hearty and brimming with flavor; side-dishes to compliment the entrées and pickles for a healthy yang finish to the main course.

Crunchy Granola

Yields: 8-10 Servings

3 cups rolled oats
¾ cup wheat germ
1/3 cup raw almonds, chopped
2 TBS shelled raw unsalted sunflower seeds
1 tsp cinnamon
¼ cup dried shredded coconut (if desired)
1 tsp sea salt
¼ cup unsweetened apple juice
¾ cup maple syrup or brown rice syrup
1 cup dried cherries, cranberries or dark raisins

Preheat oven to 325 degrees.

Combine oats, wheat germ, almonds, sunflower seeds, cinnamon, coconut and salt in a bowl.

Add apple juice and maple syrup, or brown rice syrup.

Stir well and spread the mixture evenly on a large rimmed baking sheet.

Bake, stirring every 5 minutes or so, until lightly browned (about 40 minutes).

Place baking sheet on a wire rack and cool to room temperature.

Place in a clean mixing bowl, then fold in the dried cherries, cranberries or raisins.

Allow granola to cool thoroughly and serve with plain, or vanilla rice, soy, oat or almond milk, or store in airtight containers or resealable bags.

Tip from the Chef

Homemade granola can be placed in a sealable container or plastic bag and stored at room temperature for up to 2 months. Other ingredients such as sesame oil, sesame seeds, peanuts, cashews, walnuts, currants, chopped dried apricots and vanilla can be used to create a variety of delicious granolas. Choose granola that is sweetened with fruit juice, grain syrup or maple syrup or unsweetened when purchasing packaged.

KNOW YOUR INGREDIENTS - OATS

Oats—the seeds of the cereal grain oat plant *Avena sativa*—contain more soluble fiber and protein than any other grain. Oat consumption—especially oat bran—lowers cholesterol and helps reduce the risk of heart disease. Three primary methods are used to obtain oat products; flaking, oat bran milling and whole-flour milling. The flaking process consists of passing the oat groats through steel rollers (rolled oats) to obtain oat flakes. Oat bran milling also uses rollers to produce two separate products, oat bran and de-branned oat flour, while whole flour milling grinds the whole groat into fine flour.

Tofu French Toast

Yields: 6 slices

1 cup soft tofu, drained
½ tsp cinnamon
1/8 cup unsweetened apple juice
1 TBS maple syrup
1 tsp vanilla
3 pinches of sea salt
1 TBS sesame oil for oiling the pan
6 slices whole grain sourdough bread
1 cup fresh strawberries, cut into quarters

Place tofu, cinnamon, all liquid ingredients and sea salt in a blender and blend for 3-4 minutes until smooth and creamy.

Pour blended mixture into a shallow dish.

Soak first slice of bread in mixture for 1-2 minutes.

Heat a medium size iron or stainless steel skillet, then add sesame oil.

Place bread into hot skillet and brown on both sides.

Repeat process with other bread slices.

Drizzle with hot maple syrup, brown rice syrup or lemon walnut syrup (see mochi waffle recipe on page 50), then garnish with fresh strawberries and serve.

Tip from the Chef

Flip bread over as soon as the coating browns, as it burns easily. For variety, different flavors of amasake can be substituted for the apple juice.

KNOW YOUR INGREDIENTS - ORGANIC APPLE JUICE

Unsweetened, organic apple juice is made by macerating and pressing natural-grown, pesticide-free apples. Along with the unfiltered version known as apple cider, apple juice is used more often in macrobiotic cooking than any other fruit juice.

Scrambled Tofu

Yields: 5-6 servings

1 20 oz block firm or extra firm tofu (mashed)

1 TBS of white miso

1 tsp of sesame oil

½ onion cut into small ½ inch cubes

2 pinches of sea salt

3 fresh shitake mushrooms, sliced thin

1 carrot washed and cut into small ½ inch cubes

1 ear of organic corn, removed from the cob
or ¼ cup of frozen organic corn

¼ cup of celery cut into ½ inch cubes

Place tofu in a medium-size mixing bowl and mash by hand.

Add white miso to the tofu and continue mashing until the miso is mixed well with the tofu.

Set aside. (Let sit overnight if possible).

Heat a medium-size cast iron or stainless steel skillet and add sesame oil.

When the oil is hot, add onions and sea salt, then sauté for about 3-5 minutes, or until onions are clear.

Add mushrooms and carrots and sauté 5-7 minutes until they are soft.

Add the corn and tofu mixture and mix throughly with the sautéd vegetables, then cover and simmer for 5-7 minutes.

Add celery and continue to cook for 1-2 minutes until bright green in color.

Remove from heat and serve.

Tip from the Chef

Scrambled tofu can be served at breakfast in place of scrambled eggs or used as a sandwich or wrap filling with tahini or other vegetable spread. It also works well as a filling for stuffing vegetables and pasta shells.

KNOW YOUR INGREDIENTS - SHITAKE MUSHROOMS

The shitake—available dried or fresh—is an edible mushroom cultivated on the dead logs of the Shii tree, a relative to the oak. Shitake mushrooms are commonly used to enhance the flavor of sautéd vegetar-ian dishes, soups, stews and pasta sauces. Dried Donku Shitake mushrooms—unlike the dried shitakes found in most Chinese markets—have the most medicinal value and are those most used in macrobiotic cooking.

Pancakes

Yields: 7-8 servings

1 ½ cups of whole wheat pastry flour
½ cup organic brown rice flour
¼ tsp sea salt
3 tsp non-alum baking powder
1 ½ cup of Knudsen Tangerine Spritzer
1 cup fresh blueberries, washed and drained
1 TBS sesame oil

Place dry ingredients in a mixing bowl, then mix and set aside.

Pour the spritzer into dry ingredients and using a fork, gently fold until there are no pockets of dry mix left. Do not over-beat.

Heat a large, heavy skillet or griddle over medium heat, then brush with sesame oil.

Using a ¼-cup measure, drop batter onto the skillet.

Flip pancake with a spatula when bubbles start to form on the tops and edges.

Remove from pan when golden brown on the second side.

Place maple syrup and blueberries in a small saucepan. Heat on low until the blueberries turn soft.

Drizzle on top of pancakes and serve.

Tip from the Chef

The Knudsen spritzer interacts with the baking powder and helps the pancakes rise. Non-alcoholic beer or another type of unsweetened carbonated fruit juice may be used in place of the spritzer. Batter may thicken if allowed to sit, so adjust liquid accordingly. Other fresh organic fruits may replace the blueberries in this recipe.

KNOW YOUR INGREDIENTS - BROWN RICE FLOUR

Brown rice flour, which is ground from unhulled rice kernels, adds a light crisp flavor to baked  goods and is an excellent substitute for wheat flour for those who are gluten-intolerant.

Mochi Waffles

Yields: 3-4 waffles

1 12 oz pkg of plain
or cinnamon raisin Mochi

1 TBS sesame oil

Cut mochi into thin strips.

Heat an electric or stove-top waffle iron.

Oil both sides with sesame oil.

Place cut mochi strips inside waffle iron and close to heat.

Once done, remove from iron and serve warm with maple, or Lemon Syrup.

Lemon Syrup
Yields: 3-4 servings

½ cup of brown rice syrup
1 TBS spring water

1 TBS fresh lemon juice
¼ cup walnuts- roasted and chopped fine

Place brown rice syrup, water and lemon juice in a small saucepan.
Warm over low heat and stir a little until ingredients are dissolved.
Add walnuts and serve.

Tip from the Chef

When waffle iron jaws touch, the mochi is ready. Do not overcook, as the mochi will turn from chewy to very dry and tough.

KNOW YOUR INGREDIENTS - BROWN RICE SYRUP

Brown rice syrup is a natural, thick sweetener made from a process of fermenting brown rice that is used, as an ounce-for-ounce alternative, to other liquid sweeteners such as honey and molasses. When used as an alternative to dry sweeteners, one and one-quarter cup of brown rice syrup replaces one cup of dry sweetener. However, one-quarter cup of another liquid should be removed to create the right balance.

Rice Balls

Yields: 1 serving

1 cup of cold spring water
pinch of sea salt
½ cup of cooked, short-grain organic brown rice
(see recipe for preparing brown rice, page 60)
¼ of an umeboshi plum
½ sheet of nori,
cut in half to form two equal squares

Put spring water in a bowl and add sea salt.

Stir until sea salt is disolved.

Rinse hands in the salted spring water and shake off excess.

Mold the cooked rice into a thick disc shape—similar to a do-nut without the hole—pressing firmly (ideally up to 33 times on each side) keeping hands moist to prevent rice from sticking to them.

Press the piece of umeboshi plum into the center of the rice disc.

Cover the plum completely with rice and continue to mold firmly (ideally another 33 times on each side).

Cover with nori (wet nori slightly if it doesn't cover the disc easily) and press again (ideally 33 times). (Use a little more nori if needed to cover the disc completely and do not allow any of the rice to remain exposed).

Tip from the Chef

Tightly-molded Rice Balls retain their freshness for up to a week, if covered completely with nori and kept in a cool, dry place. If rice balls are covered too tightly in saran wrap or plastic, they may become moldy. Parents in Japan send their children to school with rice balls wrapped in large, fresh bamboo leaves. You can simply wrap them in wax paper or store them in a paper bag for packed lunches.

For variety, substitute the umeboshi plum with pickles such as ginger, cucumber or daikon pickle, or omit the nori and roll the rice balls in roasted sesame seeds. Also, try pan-frying or deep-frying the rice balls in safflower oil, with, or without the nori wrap.

KNOW YOUR INGREDIENTS - NORI

Nori is harvested from the waters surrounding Japan. After being washed and spread thin to dry, nori is roasted, turning it a brilliant green while enhancing its flavor and texture. Nori is crispy in texture, with a saltiness that complements the soft sweetness of sushi rice. The Japanese eat nori almost every day, even at breakfast.

SUGGESTIONS FOR **WRAP FILLINGS**

When creating a wrap filling, balance tastes and compliment the base with fresh, roasted, grilled or pickled vegetables.

Base

Hummus, bean spreads, mashed avocado or guacomole, left over brown rice, refried beans, fried tofu, tempeh or veggie burgers.

Compliments

Fresh tomato, lettuce, cucumber, red radish, sprouts, shredded carrots, or red onions.

Grilled onions, yellow squash, zucchini, sundried tomatoes, or portobello mushrooms.

Sauerkraut or dill pickles.

Tip from the Chef

Wraps provide the convenience of an easy-to-make, hand-held meal, while offering a greater variety than the traditional sandwich and by mixing all the ingredients together first, assembly is quick.

Wraps are especially suited for those on-the-go or for kids' lunch boxes or as a simple, nutritious after-school snack. With leftovers and a little imagination, the filling combinations are endless.

Wrap Sandwich

Yields: 4 wraps

Homemade Hummus Spread
1 cup cooked or canned chickpeas
1/3 cup tahini
1/3 cup fresh parsley, chopped fine
1-2 TBS fresh lemon juice
2-3 TBS spring water
1 TBS shoyu

Grilled Vegetable Filling
3 TBS balsamic vinegar
2 tsp extra virgin olive oil
1/4 tsp sea salt
2 medium onions,
each cut crosswise into 4 pieces
2 medium zucchini,
each cut lengthwise into 4 slices
2 large bell peppers, each seeded
and cut lengthwise into 4 pieces
2 pkg (6 oz each) sliced Portobello mushrooms

Fresh Vegetable Filling
1 cucumber, sliced thin
1 tomato, sliced thin
1/4 cup of lettuce, shredded
2 medium carrots, shredded
1/2 medium red bell pepper, sliced thin
1/2 cup fresh lemon juice
2-3 TBS extra virgin olive oil

Wraps
4 large tortillas
1 bunch of watercress
2 TBS fresh basil, chopped
black pepper to taste

Prepare Homemade Hummus Spread
Combine all ingredients in a food processor or blender and blend until the mixture is smooth. (Unused hummus can be stored in the refrigerator for 5-7 days if tightly covered).

Prepare Fillings

Grilled Vegetable Filling
Preheat grill or broiler.
Add vinegar, oil and salt to a shallow baking pan and stir until well mixed.
Add onions and turn to coat.
Repeat with zucchini, peppers and mushrooms.
Place baking pan on grill rack and cook 5 minutes per side until tender, turning once and brushing with any remaining vinegar/oil/salt mixture.
Remove baking pan from grill and set aside.

Fresh Vegetable Filling
Combine cucumber, tomato, lettuce, carrots, pepper, lemon juice and olive oil in a small bowl, then set aside and allow to marinate 30 minutes before wrapping.

Create the Wrap
Spread each tortilla with 2 TBS Homemade Hummus Spread.

Place 4 watercress leaves down the center.

Top with either the Grilled Vegetable filling, or the Fresh Vegetable Filling.

Sprinkle with basil and pepper.

Roll tightly and wrap securely.

Serve immediately or wrap in plastic wrap, or foil, to take along for lunch.

KNOW YOUR INGREDIENTS - WHOLE WHEAT TORTILLA

The whole wheat tortilla is a thin, unleavened flatbread made from fine-ground, whole wheat flour. The tortilla is considered a traditional food of Mexico, but both the name (Spanish for little round cake) and the primary ingredient (wheat), were introduced to Mexico by the Spanish in the 16th century. The corn tortilla, however, was a staple food in Mexico long before the Spanish arrived.

Veggie Pizza

Yields: 1 large 12-inch pizza

Pizza Crust

3 cups unbleached white flour
3 cups whole wheat flour
½ cup corn oil
½ bottle Guiness stout
2 - 3 TBS olive oil (for rubbing bowl)
¼ cup corn meal

Pizza Sauce

2 TBS olive oil
2 cloves of garlic, finely chopped
1 small onion, finely chopped
3 pinches of sea salt
¼ tsp basil
¼ tsp oregano
¼ tsp pepper
2 cups of carrots
1¾ cups of spring water

Pizza Toppings
(see facing page)

Tip from the Chef

A bean purée or any vegetable can be used for the sauce, or pizza can be served without sauce. Carrot/beet or squash sauce are good alternatives to carrot/onion sauce. For those who prefer a tomato sauce, use diced tomatoes, crushed tomatoes or tomato paste alone or in combination and seasoned with, basil, oregano, salt, pepper, fresh garlic, fresh onion or onion powder. Add 1 teaspoon of brown rice syrup per 2 cups of sauce for a sweet taste.

Prepare the Pizza Crust

Preheat oven to 450 degrees.

Combine 1 cup of white flour and 1 cup of whole wheat flour with corn oil and beer.

Beat with a wooden spoon until the batter is smooth. Then, with floured fingers, work in enough additional flour to make soft dough that does not stick to the fingers but is not too tough to roll with a rolling pin.

Prepare work area by spreading flour on a wooden cutting board to prevent the dough from sticking when kneading.

Turn the dough onto the lightly floured board and knead for 2 minutes (about 100 kneading strokes).

Shape the dough into a ball and put it in a bowl rubbed with olive oil.

Spread the surface of dough lightly with oil, cover with a towel and let it rise until doubled in bulk, about 1½ hours.

Punch the dough down and turn onto the lightly floured board.

Place a 15-inch piece of aluminum foil on work area.

Sprinkle a little corn meal on top of aluminum foil and place the dough on the aluminum foil.

Roll the dough with a rolling pin into a 12-inch circle, then-pierce dough with a fork several times and set aside.

(continued) ✈

KNOW YOUR INGREDIENTS - OREGANO

Oregano—*Origanum vulgare*—is a perennial herb belonging to the mint family. It is also known as wild marjoram, or more commonly, "the pizza herb" because of the dish most frequently associated with it. In fact, oregano could almost be considered a "staple herb" in Italian cooking and is one of the few herbs that has a stronger flavor when dried, than when fresh. Using oregano in cooking requires a bit of caution as its warm, pungent, slightly-bitter taste can easily overpower other flavors.

Prepare the Pizza Sauce

Place olive oil in pan and warm on medium heat for one or two minutes.

Add garlic and onion and sauté (take care not to brown the garlic and make it bitter).

Add salt, basil, oregano and pepper (if making for young children, seasonings can be omitted).

Add carrots and spring water and cover.

Cook for 20 minutes on low heat.

Let cool a few minutes and then purée in a food mill or blender.

Putting it all together

Spread sauce generously on pizza crust.

Add toppings (see above right).

Place pizza in oven and bake for approximately 15 minutes.

PIZZA TOPPINGS MIX AND MATCH

Any combination of:

Fresh Vegetables
- orange, yellow, red, or green peppers
- mushrooms
- onions or scallions
- spinach
- broccoli

Chop, slice, or dice the vegetables (sauté in a little olive oil before adding them to the pizza for an even nicer flavor).

Fresh Herbs
- chives
- parsley
- fresh garlic
- minced celery leaves

Miscellaneous
- sautéd seitan
- fried tempeh strip
- nori flakes
- olives

Cheese Alternatives
- finely grated mochi
- mochi marinated in white miso and water
- fresh tofu
- tofu fermented with white miso
- soy or rice cheese.

Soy or rice cheese should be used infrequently as they are made with dairy products.

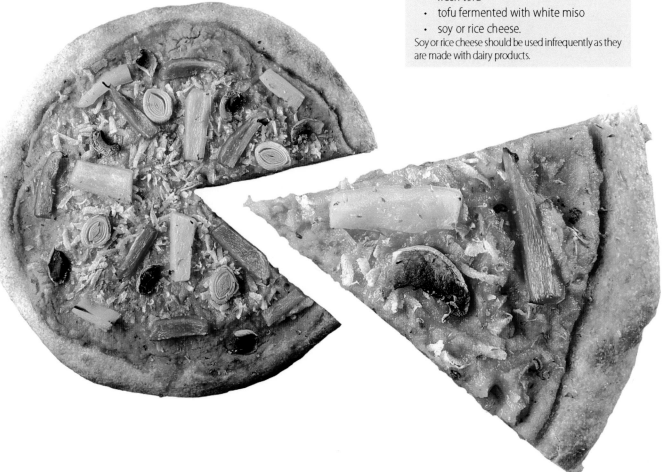

Bean-Filled Tacos

Yields: 5-6 tacos

1 TBS extra virgin olive oil
1 small onion, minced
2 cloves garlic, minced
1 bell pepper, chopped fine
2 cups of fresh-cooked beans
(or one 14½-oz can), mashed
(black, pink, red, or pinto beans work best)
2 TBS yellow cornmeal
1 ½ TBS cumin
1 tsp paprika
1 tsp cayenne pepper
1 tsp chili powder
1 cup salsa
Vegan taco shells or warmed, soft corn tortillas

Heat skillet over medium heat, then add olive oil.

Stir in onion, garlic and bell pepper; cook until tender.

Stir in the mashed beans and cornmeal.

Mix in cumin, paprika, cayenne, chili powder and salsa.

Cover and cook 5 minutes.

If using soft taco shells, steam briefly to soften.

Fill vegan taco shells or soft corn tortillas with a generous amount of filling and serve.

Tip from the Chef

The tacos may be garnished with guacamole, shredded lettuce, sprouts, onion, or crumbled tofu cheese.
The bean filling can also be used for making burritos, or simply as a delicious dip for tortilla chips.

KNOW YOUR INGREDIENTS - CORN TORTILLA

The corn tortilla has been a staple food in Mexico and Central America for thousands of years. The Aztecs called it *tlaxcalli*. When the Spanish arrived in Mexico the 16th century, they christened it "little round cake"—tortilla. Corn tortillas are made by mixing fine-ground cornmeal with water to form a dough known as masa. The dough is then shaped into golf-ball size pieces, patted down by hand to make a thin pancake shape and placed onto a hot griddle and cooked on both sides.

Black Bean Burger

Yields: 4-6 servings

1½ cups cooked brown rice, mashed
1 cup cooked black beans, mashed
½ cup carrot, finely grated
½ cup onion, finely grated
¼ cup tahini
2 TBS shoyu
1 TBS parsley
¼ tsp basil
¼ tsp thyme
2 TBS sesame seeds
¼ cup organic whole wheat flour
4-6 whole grain hamburger buns
ketchup and mustard as desired

Garnish
tomato, sliced
onion, sliced into thin rings
dill pickle, sliced
lettuce, shredded or leaf

Mix cooked rice in a bowl with a hand blender until well-mashed.

Stir in mashed cooked beans, onions and carrots with a wooden spoon, then stir in tahini, shoyu and spices.

Add enough flour to keep the mixture together (adjust the amount of flour if necessary).

Shape into round patties.

Heat a cast-iron skillet.

Add oil and patty, then brown patty on both sides (5-7 min each side).

Open buns and place on serving plates.

Place patty on bottom half of whole grain bun.

Spread top half of whole grain bun with ketchup and mustard.

Garnish burger with tomato, onion and dill pickle slices and shredded or leaf lettuce.

Place top half of whole grain bun on burger and serve.

Tip from the Chef

Make sure patties are dry enough to hold together firmly, otherwise they will fall apart in the frying pan during cooking.

KNOW YOUR INGREDIENTS - BLACK BEANS

Black beans—often called turtle beans—are small oval-shaped legumes that have a shiny black shell, a dense, meaty texture and a slight mushroom-like flavor. Black beans belong to the same species—*Phaseolus vulgaris* (common bean)—as the pinto, kidney, white and other popular beans. The black bean is a frequent ingredient in Latin American cooking and the history of its use there, dates back some 7,000 years. They are also a frequent ingredient in vegetarian diets due to their high nutritional value, especially when combined with a whole grain like brown rice. Black Turtle Beans should not be confused with Japanese Black Soybeans which are also highly nutritious and used in macrobiotic cooking as well.

Tempeh Reuben

Yields: 3 servings

8-oz package of tempeh, cut into thirds
1 TBS shoyu
1 cup of spring water
1-inch piece of kombu
1 TBS sesame seed oil
½ cup of sauerkraut
1 large onion, cut to match the thickness of sauerkraut
1 cup lettuce, torn into bite size pieces
¼ cup mochi, finely grated
6 slices of whole grain rye sourdough bread

Thousand Island Dressing
Yields: 1½ cup

12 oz silken tofu	1 tsp shoyu
1 TBS organic ketchup	1 tsp mustard
1 TBS dill pickle, diced	1 TBS rice syrup

Blend all ingredients in a blender until creamy.

Tip from the Chef

Tempeh can last up to 3 months if stored frozen in its original packaging. It can be defrosted quickly by placing under warm running water, though once defrosted, tempeh should be used within a day or so.

Heat a cast-iron skillet, then add tempeh pieces and brown for 3-4 minutes on each side.

Remove tempeh from skillet and set aside.

Place shoyu, spring water and kombu in a saucepan, then cover and bring to a boil.

Add tempeh, lower heat to simmer and cook for 20 minutes.

Heat a cast-iron skillet, then add sesame oil and onion and sauté onion until slightly brown, about 10 minutes.

Remove tempeh from kombu-shoyu broth and add to the skillet with the onion, then cover and steam for 10 minutes.

Add sauerkraut and grated mochi to the tempeh and onion, cover and steam for 5 minutes.

Prepare Thousand Island Dressing (see left).

Steam three slices of rye sourdough bread in a bamboo or stainless steel steamer for 3-4 minutes.

Place three slices of steamed bread on individual plates.

Place temphe on bread slices. Cover with lettuce and add a layer of the onion/sauerkraut/mochi mixture, then spread thousand island dressing on top.

Cover with a dry slice of bread and serve.

KNOW YOUR INGREDIENTS - TEMPEH

Tempeh is a fermented food product made by a natural culturing and controlled fermentation process that binds soybeans into cake form. A staple source of protein in Indonesia, tempah is often used as a meat substitute and is sometimes known as, "Javanese meat". Like tofu, tempeh is made from soybeans, but unlike tofu, it is a whole soybean product with a higher content of protein, dietary fiber and vitamins. Tempeh has a firmer texture and stronger flavor than tofu and because of the fermentation, is more digestible. Tempeh has a nutty, meaty and mushroom-like flavor.

Falafels
with Tahini Sauce

Yields: 4 servings

11/3 cups of chickpeas, freshly cooked or canned
2 cloves of garlic, crushed
1 tsp ground coriander
1 tsp ground cumin
1 TBS fresh parsley, chopped
2 scallions, finely chopped
1 tsp or more tahini
¼ cup of roasted tan sesame seeds
3 TBS sesame oil
1 cup of red leaf lettuce, torn into bite size pieces
2 large whole wheat pita pockets-sliced in half
1 scallion for garnish
4 red radishes sliced

Make Falafels

Combine chickpeas with garlic, spices, herbs, scallions and seasonings and blend in a food processor until the mixture forms a coarse paste. (Add more tahini if needed).

With slightly wet hands, form mixture into small patties, then coat with toasted sesame seeds.

Heat sesame oil in a large frying pan and fry the falafel over low heat for 10-15 minutes, turning once.

Fill Pita Pockets

Open pita pockets and place on serving plates, then insert lettuce, red radish and falafel patties.

Garnish with a sliced scallion.

Tahini Sauce can either be added to the pita pocket or used separately as a dip.

Tahini Sauce

Yields: ¾ cup

½ cup tahini	1 tsp brown rice vinegar
1 TBS shoyu	1 tsp cayenne pepper
1 TBS lemon juice	1 scallion, finely sliced

Mix ingredients thoroughly in a small mixing bowl.

Tip from the Chef

To toast sesame seeds, first rinse under cold water in a fine-mesh strainer then place in a hot, cast-iron frying pan. Stir often to prevent burning. To test if sesame seeds are thoroughly toasted; scoop up a spoonful and then turn spoon upside down. If the seeds fall off the spoon, they are properly toasted.

KNOW YOUR INGREDIENTS - TAN SESAME SEEDS

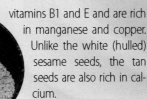

Tan sesame seeds are a variety of the unhulled pod seeds of the sesame plant—*Sesamum indicum*. They are a good source of vitamins B1 and E and are rich in manganese and copper. Unlike the white (hulled) sesame seeds, the tan seeds are also rich in calcium.

KNOW YOUR INGREDIENTS - BROWN RICE

Brown rice is obtained from milling the seeds of the rice plant Oryza sativa. A rice huller removes the outer husks of the grain (chaff) and the rice at this point, is known as brown rice. If processed further by removing the bran and the germ, the product is called white rice. Whole-grain brown rice contains the exact same proportion of protein, water, fat, minerals and carbohydrates as the human body, which makes it a balanced food to eat on a daily basis. In fact, brown rice is often served as a main course in a macrobiotic diet as it provides a great source of complex carbohydrates and easily compliments beans and vegetable side dishes.

Basic Brown Rice

Yields: 3-4 servings

1 cup short-grain organic brown rice
1½ cups spring water
3 pinches of sea salt or
a 1-inch strip of kombu sea vegetable

Tip from the Chef

Because pressure-cooking retains all the steam and heat within the pot, rice prepared in a pressure cooker has a more satisfying flavor and is more digestible. In addition, more vitamins and minerals are retained during pressure-cooking than with conventional cooking methods. The magic of pressure-cooking is that any grain or bean added to the brown rice in the pressure cooker will take exactly the same time to cook as the rice—45 minutes! Be creative: add ½ cup of any grain, presoaked beans, toasted nuts, or seeds to this recipe. (Make sure to add additional spring water as needed to maintain a ratio of 1 cup of ingredients to 1½ cups of water). If adding beans or dried chestnuts, presoak them overnight in a separate bowl from the rice. Additional grains can be soaked with the rice after it has been washed. Toasted seeds and nuts can just be added to the pressure cooker with the rice.

Place brown rice into a bowl, then add enough water to cover the rice and stir with your hands until dust and dirt start to rise to the surface of the water.

Strain rice through a strainer and repeat washing process twice.

Place rice into a clean bowl, then cover with 1½ cups of spring water and soak at least 2-3 hours, preferably overnight.

To boil rice (if pressure-cooking the rice, skip to pressure-cooking, below):
Add salt or kombu to the rice and soaking water, then pour the mixture into a 4-quart saucepan and bring to a boil.

Lower heat and simmer for 45 minutes. If the rice becomes too dry during cooking, add a little more water to prevent the rice at the bottom of the pan from burning.

Remove rice from saucepan with a wooden spoon and place into a serving bowl to cool.

To pressure-cook rice:
Add salt or kombu to the rice and soaking water, then pour the mixture into a 5-quart pressure cooker.

Close and lock the pressure lid and bring up to pressure over medium-high heat.

If cooking with gas:
After the pressure comes up, place a flame tamer under the pressure cooker. Make sure the pressure returns to the proper level after you put the flame tamer under the pressure cooker; if it does not, turn the flame a little higher.

Set timer, cook for 45 minutes, then turn off heat.

After the pressure has dropped, open the pressure cooker and spoon rice into a bowl to cool.

ADDITIONAL SUGGESTIONS FOR BROWN RICE

Simple and nutritious one-dish meals can be created by adding cooked corn, beans, nuts, vegetables and seeds to cooked brown rice. Soups, vegetable stews and stir fries can be enhanced with the nutty flavor of brown rice, which will also add a nice texture. Use leftover brown rice to make a pan-fried burger; add beans or tofu to the rice or just form into small balls and deep fry. Brown rice is a good substitute for white rice in recipes and a healthy alternative.

Vegetarian Lasagna

Yields: 8-10 servings

6-oz package of
organic durum semolina lasagna noodles

¼ cup of spring water

1 cup onions, cut into ½-inch cubes

4 pinches of sea salt

6 cups carrots, cut into 1-inch cubes

1 beet, cut into 1-inch cubes

1 fresh bay leaf

1 TBS barley miso, diluted in a few TBS of spring water

1 20-oz package of soft tofu

1 umeboshi plum

1 TBS + 1 tsp extra virgin olive oil

1 cup broccoli, cut into small flowerets

1 cup fresh button mushrooms

¼ cup fresh basil

1 TBS shoyu

1 tsp oregano

1 tsp umeboshi vinegar

½ cup finely grated mochi

Prepare the sauce

Fill a 6-quart pan with spring water and bring to a boil.

Add lasagna noodles and boil for 8-10 minutes.

Drain noodles in a colander, rinse with cold water and set aside.

Coat the bottom of a 4-quart saucepan with 1 TBS of spring water, then add onions and 1 pinch of sea salt.

Sauté until onions are clear and lightly browned.

Add carrots, beet, 3 pinches of sea salt and fresh bay leaf, then add the rest of the ¼ cup of spring water.

Cover the pot and bring to boil, then lower heat, cover and simmer for 25-30 minutes until carrots and beets are soft.

Season with 1 TBS of diluted barley miso.

Spoon cooked carrot mixture into a blender and blend until smooth, then pour into a bowl and set aside.

Blend the soft tofu in a food processor with the umeboshi plum until smooth and set aside.

Heat a cast-iron skillet, then add olive oil and stir-fry broccoli and mushrooms.

Season with shoyu, fresh basil, oregano and ume vinegar.

(continued)

Tip from the Chef

Various combinations of vegetables can also be cooked together and then blended to make a pasta sauce: onions and tomatoes; onion and carrots; onions, carrots and tomatoes; onions, carrots and squash (Hokkaido, butternut or buttercup); or onions, carrots, squash and beets (beets will give the lasagna sauce a sweet flavor and a vibrant red color).

KNOW YOUR INGREDIENTS - DURUM SEMOLINA PASTA

Durum semolina pasta is made from the semolina obtained from the milling of durum wheat. Durum—the Latin word for hard—is, as the name implies, a very hard wheat from which a very hard semolina—a prerequisite for making high quality pasta—is obtained. Unlike pasta made from soft wheat semolina, durum semolina pasta does not clump or become sticky when cooked.

Prepare the lasagna
Preheat oven to 375 degrees.

Coat a 9-inch-square baking dish with 1 tsp of olive oil.

Spread ¼ cup of the carrot-onion sauce on the bottom of
    the oiled baking dish and cover with noodles, then lay-
    er with stir-fried vegetables, tofu cream, grated mochi,
    sauce and noodles.

Repeat process until ingredients are all used.

Cover final layer with sauce and grated mochi.

Cover dish and bake for 30 minutes until brown on top and
    mochi has melted throughout the dish.

Cut into squares while still warm and serve.

Chinese-Style Stir-Fry

Yields: 6-8 servings

1 TBS dark sesame oil
1 small onion, diced
½ cup of lotus root, diced
pinch of sea salt
4 shiitake mushrooms, soaked and cut thin
1 stalk of celery, sliced thin on the diagonal
1½ cups Chinese cabbage, sliced thin on the diagonal
1 cup of bean sprouts
3 cups of spring water
3 TBS of kuzu (dissolved in ¼ cup of spring water)

Heat wok or skillet, then brush with oil.

Add onions and sauté until clear.

Add lotus root and a pinch of sea salt and sauté for 1-2 minutes.

Add shiitake mushrooms, cabbage, celery and sprouts in that order, sautéing for 1-2 minutes after each addition. Keep the veggies moving with cooking chop sticks or a wooden spoon.

Add spring water; cover and bring to a boil, then lower heat and simmer for 2-3 minutes.

Remove veggies when they are cooked thoroughly, though still crunchy and place in a bowl. (Keep cooking liquid in the pan).

Turn off heat and add diluted kuzu to the cooking liquid, then stir until thick.

Pour liquid over the vegetables, mix thoroughly and serve over cooked noodles or brown rice.

Tip from the Chef

To make Chinese-style stir-fried veggies you can use any thinly sliced root, round, or leafy green veggies. Heat oil or water in skillet. Add roots first with a pinch of sea salt or a dash of shoyu. Then add the rounds and leafy greens.

KNOW YOUR INGREDIENTS - CHINESE CABBAGE

Chinese cabbage actually comes in two different varieties. The light green broad-leaved *Brassica rapa Pekinensis*, also known as napa cabbage or snow cabbage, forms a long cylindrical head  and is the variety commonly known as Chinese cabbage. The other, *Brassica rapa Chinensis*, has darker leaves, does not form a head and is commonly known as bok choy or Chinese mustard.

Tofu Nori Rolls

Yields: 3 servings

1 cup of spring water
2 dried shiitake mushrooms
1 tsp sesame oil
1 carrot, cut into match sticks
2 tsp shoyu
1 tsp mirin
8-oz block of extra-firm tofu, mashed
½ tsp mustard
3 sheets of nori

Soak mushrooms for 20 minutes in spring water. Remove from water and discard the stems. Slice mushrooms.

Heat a saucepan. Add sesame oil and sauté mushrooms and carrots until soft.

Season with mirin and shoyu.

Place tofu into a mixing bowl and then mash by hand.

Fold in cooked carrots and mushrooms with a wooden spoon, then stir in mustard.

Place one sheet of nori, shiny side up, on a bamboo mat.

Place a ¼-inch layer of tofu mixture one inch from the closest edge of the sushi mat.

Roll the nori tightly around the tofu mixture.

Unwrap mat from nori roll and then repeat, rolling to complete, making all three rolls.

Place the rolls in the steamer, then cover and steam for 15-20 minutes.

Remove and cool.

Cut rolls into 1-inch slices and serve.

Tip from the Chef

Drain off any excess liquid from the tofu mixture as it may weaken the nori covering during steaming. Bamboo steamers work best to keep the outside of the rolls dry while steaming.

KNOW YOUR INGREDIENTS - MIRIN

Mirin is a sweet tasting, low-alcohol content cooking wine made from rice. Because the sweet taste—different from that of sug-ar—is very strong, mirin should be used sparingly. A small amount will enhance the flavor of any dish. In Japan, mirin is also considered a ceremonial drink and is used to usher in the New Year.

Bubbling Barley Stew

Yields: 4-6 servings

2 dried shiitake mushrooms
1 cup of spring water
1 TBS sesame oil
½ block (4 oz) firm tofu, sliced
2 medium onions, sliced into half-moons
3 pinches of sea salt
1 cup pearl barley
4 cups of spring water
¼ cup lotus root, sliced into ½-inch rounds
and then cut into ¼-inch pieces
1 large carrot, cut into ½-inch cubes
2 stalks celery, cut into ½-inch cubes
¼ cup of leeks, sliced on the diagonal
1 TBS barley miso diluted in 1 TBS spring water
2 TBS parsley, chopped fine

Soak mushrooms for 20 minutes in 1 cup of spring water, then remove, discard stems and slice. (Save soaking water for later use).

Heat a large frying pan, add sesame oil and fry both sides of the tofu slices.

Drain excess oil from tofu, then cut into ¼-inch strips and set aside.

Drain any excess oil from the pan and sauté onions with one pinch of sea salt for 3-4 minutes until onions are slightly limp and brown, then set aside.

Place barley and 2 pinches of sea salt into a pan with 4 cups of spring water.

Cover and bring to boil, then lower heat and simmer for 1/2 hour.

Add lotus root, carrot, mushrooms and soaking water (from step 1), then cover and cook for 1 hour.

Stir in celery, leeks and fried tofu.

Lightly season with diluted miso and simmer 3-4 minutes, then add the sautéd onions.

Serve warm with a garnish of chopped parsley.

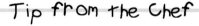

Tip from the Chef

The Japanese Hato mugi barley—also known as Job's Tears—may be used instead of pearl barley.

KNOW YOUR INGREDIENTS - PEARL BARLEY

Pearl barley is cereal grain from the grass plant—*Hordeum vulgare*—which has been processed to remove its hull and part of the bran. Pearl barley is less nutritious than barley that has only been hulled, but retaining the bran makes barley tough and chewy.

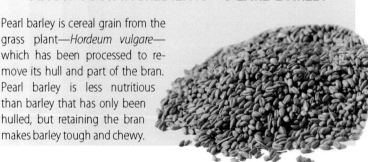

Deep Fried Tofu Stew

Yields: 6-8 servings

8-oz block of extra-firm tofu,
cut into 1-inch cubes

2 cups safflower oil

2 cups of root and round vegetables,
cut to match the tofu cubes

1 TBS shoyu

1 TBS kuzu powder

Pour safflower oil into a 5-quart, cast-iron pot or sauce pan, then heat uncovered.

After a minute or two, test the oil by dropping in a small piece of tofu.

- If it falls to the bottom of the pot and slowly rises to the top and bubbles, the oil is ready.
- If it falls to the bottom and stays there, the oil is too cool.
- If it falls to the bottom and quickly rises to the top, the oil is too hot.

Adjust the heat accordingly.

Drop tofu cubes in hot oil, several pieces at a time and cook until lightly brown, then remove, drain on a paperbag and set aside.

Layer root and round vegetables in a heavy, lidded saucepan, then add 1 inch of water.

Add tofu, cover pan and bring to a boil.

Reduce heat to low and simmer for 30-40 minutes until the mixture becomes soft and reaches the consistency of a stew.

Remove the vegetables and tofu from the pan.

Dissolve kuzu in ¼ cup of cold water, then slowly add to whatever liquid is left in the saucepan and season with shoyu.

Stir vegetables and tofu into sauce, then ladle into soup bowls and serve.

Tip from the Chef

Deep-frying tofu before adding it to the stew creates a richer taste than simply adding plain tofu. Deep-fried tofu can also be added to grain or noodle dishes or soups to provide a richer taste. When deep-fried tofu is served alone in Japanese restaurants, it is called "age dashi tofu" and is accompanied by a dipping sauce of shoyu and daikon to help with the digestion of oil. Deep-fried tempeh can be substituted for the deep-fried tofu.

KNOW YOUR INGREDIENTS - SHOYU

Shoyu is the Japanese word for soy sauce, but not all soy sauces are shoyu. They all start with the same base — soybeans packed in salt and fermented with the mold koji—but to become true shoyu, wheat needs to be added to the process. The best shoyu are those that have been naturally aged for several years.

Tofu Quiche

Yields: 8 servings

Crust
½ cup whole-wheat pastry flour
½ cup cornmeal flour
¼ teaspoon salt
1 TBS olive oil
1-2 tsp iced spring water

Filling
1 TBS sesame seed oil
1 medium-size onion, diced
¼ cup broccoli, chopped fine
¼ cup of fresh shiitake mushrooms
3 scallions, chopped fine
1 tsp shoyu
1 20-oz package of soft tofu, crumbled
1 TBS white miso
½ cup mochi, finely shredded

Tip from the Chef

Mixing either dark or light miso with tofu creates a nice, cheesy flavor. The longer it is left to ferment, the stronger the cheese flavor.

Prepare the Crust
Preheat oven to 350° F.

Mix dry ingredients for the crust in a mixing bowl, then using a fork, stir the oil mixture slowly into the flour mixture until it is crumbly.

Gradually stir in enough ice water so that the dough will hold together.

Knead the dough in the bowl a few times, then place the dough between sheets of parchment paper and roll into a 12-inch circle.

Remove the top sheet and turn the dough into a 9-inch pie pan.

Prepare the Filling
Heat a frying pan. Add oil. Sauté onions until they are lightly browned, then add broccoli, mushrooms, scallions and shoyu.

Sauté until broccoli is bright in color (5-7 minutes) and set aside. (Add a little water if needed to prevent burning).

Place tofu and white miso in a blender and blend until creamy, then stir in mochi with a spoon.

Assemble and Bake the Quiche
Spread stir-fried vegetable mixture over the bottom of the pie crust, then carefully cover with tofu mixture.

Bake the quiche until a knife inserted in the center comes out clean, 25-30 minutes.

Let cool on a wire rack for 10-15 minutes before serving.

KNOW YOUR INGREDIENTS - OLIVE OIL

Olive oil is obtained by pressing the fruit of the olive tree—*Olea europaea*. If the oil was extracted, using only physical means and no chemical treatment, it is called virgin olive oil, otherwise it is called refined. Extra virgin olive oil is virgin olive oil that meets certain stringent criteria, regarding low acidity, taste, color and aroma. Olive oil can be used as a substitute for corn oil in baking but should not be used for deep frying.

Seitan Stroganoff with Tofu Sour Cream

Yields: 5-6 servings

1 TBS extra virgin olive oil
1 medium onion, cut into half-moon slices
8-oz package of seitan
¼ lb of organic, button mushrooms, sliced thin
2 TBS spring water
2 tsp of shoyu
1 tsp almond butter
2 tsp tahini
1 TBS fresh parsley, minced
1 package of udon noodles, cooked and rinsed
(or 2 cups cooked brown rice)

Heat a large frying pan, add 1 TBS olive oil and sauté onions until they are golden brown.

Add seitan and cook for 5 additional minutes.

Add mushrooms, 2 TBS spring water and shoyu, then cover pan and simmer for 20 minutes.

Mix tahini and almond butter in a small bowl, then pour over seitan and simmer for another 5-7 minutes.

Add parsley at the very end of cooking.

Serve seitan over pasta or rice with a scoop of tofu sour cream.

Tofu Sour Cream

Yields: 2 cups

20-oz block of soft tofu, mashed
1 tsp umeboshi vinegar
1 tsp brown rice vinegar
1 tsp spring water

Place tofu, umeboshi vinegar, brown rice vinegar and water into a blender and blend until smooth.

Tip from the Chef

Nut butters and tahini can be used in place of dairy foods to add a rich, oily flavor to dishes. Tahini comes in light and dark varieties. The former is made from unroasted tan sesame seeds; the latter from roasted tan sesame seeds. Almond butter also comes from roasted or unroasted almonds, with the roasted being easier to digest.

KNOW YOUR INGREDIENTS - SEITAN

Seitan is the name used to refer to wheat gluten in macrobiotic cuisine and is said to have been coined by the founder of the macrobiotic movement, George Ohsawa. Wheat gluten is obtained by dissolving away the starch in wheat flour with water. It is often used as a meat-substitute alternative to soy-based meat imitations, like temeph and tofu.

Miraculous Millet Mash

Yields: 6-8 servings

1 cup millet

1 head of cauliflower, chopped into small 1-inch pieces

4 cups spring water

1 tsp sea salt

Rinse millet and place in a large saucepan and add chopped cauliflower, spring water and sea salt.

Cover pan and bring to boil, then lower heat and simmer for 50 minutes.

When fully cooked, place in a Foley Food Mill or food processor and blend until consistency is similar to mashed potatoes.

Serve topped with mushroom gravy.

Mushroom Gravy

Yields: 4 cups

2 TBS sesame oil

1 large onion, diced

2 cups fresh mushrooms, sliced

4 cups spring water

3 TBS shoyu

5 TBS kuzu, dissolved in cold water

1 TBS chopped parsley

Heat large skillet and add oil, then sauté onions until lightly browned.

Add mushrooms and cook for 2 minutes over medium-low heat, then add water and shoyu and stir.

Remove from heat and allow to cool, then stir in dissolved kuzu and cook on low, stirring constantly until thick and clear.

Add parsley and pour into a serving bowl.

Tip from the Chef

Millet and cauliflower can also be pressure cooked for 45 minutes. Adjust consistency of the mashed millet or gravy by adding more or less spring water.

KNOW YOUR INGREDIENTS - MILLET

Millet is the small, roundish seed of any of several grass varieties known by the collective name, the millets. At least five varieties are in commercial production. Millet helps the spleen and pancreas to relax and regulate blood sugar.

Green Rolls

Yields: 1 roll

4 cups spring water
1 pinch of sea salt
3 large collard greens
3 medium-size rutabaga slices
1 TBS sauerkraut,
rinsed to remove excess salt
1 TBS roasted pumpkin seeds,
finely chopped
1 tsp plain mustard

As seen on:

Sheri-Lynn DeMaris

Place spring water and sea salt in a medium-size saucepan, then cover and bring to a boil.

Lightly blanch collard greens by dipping them in boiling water.

Remove with a vegetable skimmer when the leaves are bright green in color and set aside on a plate to cool.

Repeat blanching with the rutabaga slices and set aside on a plate to cool.

Lay out a clean bamboo mat and completely cover with collard greens, alternating horizontally in layers.

Place the sauerkraut, rutabaga and chopped pumpkin seeds horizontally on the collard greens, one inch from the closest edge of the sushi mat.

Spread a thin layer of mustard on top of the filling.

Roll tightly (keep the sushi mat on the outside of the roll), then squeeze the mat to remove excess water.

Remove sushi mat and place green roll lengthwise onto cutting board.

Moisten knife and slice carefully into 5-6 even pieces and serve.

Tip from the Chef

Chinese cabbage can also be used for green rolls. Other filling ideas include: nori, watercress, umeboshi paste, tahini, any blanched or round vegetable, toasted sunflower seeds, sesame seeds, almonds or walnuts, pickled cucumbers or ginger.

KNOW YOUR INGREDIENTS - COLLARD GREENS

Collard greens are the leaves of the collard plant, which belong to the same species—*Brassica oleracea*—as cabbage and broccoli. A staple vegetable of southern cooking, collard greens are a good source of vitamin C and soluble fiber. They also contain nutrients with strong anti-cancer properties. Because the leaves resemble folded money, collard greens are traditionally eaten on New Year's Day to ensure wealth in the coming year.

Kinpira

Yields: 4 servings

2 shitake mushrooms, soaked in ¼ cup spring water

1 TBS light sesame oil

½ cup burdock, sliced into thin matchsticks

½ cup carrots, sliced into thin matchsticks

½ cup lotus root, sliced into thin rounds and then quarter each round

1 TBS shoyu

1 tsp mirin

1 TBS toasted sesame seeds

Soak dried shitake mushrooms in ¼ cup spring water for 20 minutes, then slice thin and set aside. (Save soaking water).

Heat a stainless steel or cast iron frying pan and add sesame oil.

Add burdock and sauté for a couple of minutes, then add carrots and lotus root and sauté for 5 minutes.

Add mushroom soaking water to half-cover the vegetables, then add sliced mushrooms and bring to boil.

Reduce heat to low, cover pan and simmer 30 minutes.

Remove cover, season with shoyu and continue cooking with the cover off for 5-7 minutes.

When water has been cooked off, stir in mirin, fold in sesame seeds and serve.

Tip from the Chef

A ¼ cup of dried tofu, soaked and thinly sliced or other hearty root or round vegetables may be added for variety. Spring water may be used in place of oil.

Open Sesame Arame

Yields: 3-4 servings

½ cup of arame seaweed, rinsed

3-4 TBS spring water

¼ cup of sauerkraut

2 tsp of sesame tahini

1 TBS of scallions, sliced thin

Place rinsed arame in a small saucepan and add spring water to cover, then cover pan and simmer for 15-20 minutes.

Fold in sauerkraut, add tahini and simmer for 5-7 more minutes.

Turn off heat and fold in scallions and serve.

Tip from the Chef

Arame can be replaced with hiziki, but it must be rinsed and then soaked for about 15 minutes and cooked a little longer before adding tahini and sauerkraut.

Azuki Bean Delight
Yields: 5-6 servings

1 cup azuki beans	1 cup winter squash
½ cup dried chestnuts	(Butternut, Buttercup or Hokkaido pumpkin)
2 ½ cups of spring water	cut into 1-inch chunks
1-inch piece of kombu	3 pinches of sea salt

Soak azuki beans in 1 ½ cups spring water and chestnuts in 1 cup of spring water for 4-5 hours or overnight.

Put kombu in the bottom of a large saucepan, add beans, chestnuts and soaking water, then cover pan and boil.

Lower heat and simmer for 30 minutes.

Add squash and continue cooking for 20 minutes or until beans and chestnuts are soft.

Add sea salt and cook for 10 minutes until any excess cooking water has evaporated and serve.

Tip from the Chef

After the last step, this dish can be turned into a nice squash pudding by adding 1 teaspoon of tahini, 1 tablespoon barley malt and 2 tablespoons of dried dark raisins or currents. Simmer for 10 minutes and mash mixture in a Foley Food Mill or similar device.

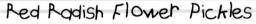

Red Radish Flower Pickles
Yields: 4 radish flowers

1 cup-size glass jar	1/8 cup of umeboshi vinegar
7/8 cup of spring water	4 red radishes

Pour water into jar, then add umeboshi vinegar.

Slice bottom of radishes so they stand up straight on the cutting board.

Align two chopsticks horizontally along either side of the radish and make 3 evenly spaced verticle cuts. (Chopsticks prevent the knife from cutting entirely through radish).

Turn radish and make 3 more cuts to create a criss cross design on top.

Place cut radishes in pickle brine, then cover jar with cheesecloth and store in a dark, cool place for 3 days.

After 3 days, put jar in refrigerator to stop the pickling.

Tip from the Chef

Pickles will keep for 2-4 days. Shoyu can be used in place of the umeboshi vinegar and other vegetables can replace the radishes. When pickling various types of vegetables together, heartier vegetables should be placed on the bottom and tender, softer vegetables, should be on top.

Green Medley
Yields: 2-3 servings

4 cups of spring water
1-2 pinches of sea salt

1 cup of different kinds chopped fresh
green leafy vegetables

Place spring water and sea salt in a large-size saucepan, then cover and bring to boil.

Boil greens one type at a time and remove with a vegetable skimmer when bright in color.

Add chopped roasted seeds or nuts, rinsed sauerkraut, cooked shitake mushrooms or other cooked vegetables and serve.

Tip from the Chef

Some greens take a very short time to cook (under 1 minute) while other heartier greens take longer (about 3-5 minutes).

Pixie Dill Pickles
Yields: 3-4 servings

5 cups spring water
3 TBS sea salt
½ cup minced onion

2 TBS fresh dill, chopped
5 small Kirby cucumbers

Place spring water in a medium-size saucepan, then add sea salt and bring to boil.

Turn heat to low and stir until sea salt dissolves, then add onion and dill and simmer for 1-2 minutes.

Remove from heat and allow to cool.

Pour mixture in a glass jar or ceramic pickle crock.

Add cucumbers. (Be sure vegetables are completely covered with liquid).

Cover jar with cheesecloth and store in a dark, cool place for 3 days. (If white foam develops on top of the jar, scoop off and replace with a clean, dry piece of cheesecloth).

After 3 days, stop pickling process by placing jar in the refrigerator and cover with a lid.

Remove pickles and rinse off excess salt before eating.

Tip from the Chef

Cucumbers can be replaced with broccoli, carrots, daikon, red radish, cauliflower, turnip, rutabaga or watermelon rind. Brines can be made from salt water, shoyu and water, or umeboshi and water and seasoned with lemon, ginger or brown rice vinegar. Vary pickling time according to size of vegetables. Refrigerated vegetables will keep up to 3-4 weeks. The brine can be saved and reused.

Sensational Salads

Salads can be created to complement a meal or to eat as an entrée. They can be packed up for travel as long as they are stored in a cool place. When storing salads, keep the dressing separate or it will create a soggy dish. Included are a wide variety of salad recipes. Some consist only of fresh greens and vegetables and fruits from the garden; other salads include a protein, sea vegetables and/or grain products.

Mock Caesar Salad

Yields: 3-4 servings

Salad Ingredients

2 bunches of romaine lettuce,
cut into bite size pieces

1 cup croutons
(toasted whole wheat bread cut into cubes)

Tofu Dressing

12.3 oz pkg of silken tofu
3 TBS fresh lemon juice
1 garlic clove, pressed
2 TBS tahini
2 tsp yellow mustard
1 TBS extra virgin olive oil
2 tsp shoyu
2 TBS fresh parsley chopped fine

Place the romaine pieces and croutons in a salad bowl.

Combine all the ingredients for the dressing, except the olive oil, in a separate bowl.

Add the olive oil in a thin stream, whisking constantly until well blended and smooth.

Pour dressing over the salad and serve.

Tip from the Chef

To help make the dressing more digestible, heat the oil first in a small saucepan on the stove and allow to cool. Eating raw oil is very hard on the liver. Adding lemon juice and sea salt to raw oil helps it become a little bit easier to digest.

KNOW YOUR INGREDIENTS - SILKEN TOFU

Silken tofu has a softer consistency than regular tofu, which makes it ideal to use for creating thick, creamy textured salad dressings, sauces and desserts.
Silken tofu is usually packaged in boxes that—unlike regular tofu—do not require refrigeration.

Blanched Daikon Salad with Plum Dressing

Yields: 4-5 servings

Salad Ingredients

4 cups of spring water

2 pinches of sea salt

1 large daikon, cut into matchsticks, ¼ inch-thick pieces on the diagonal

1 large carrot, cut into matchsticks, ¼ inch-thick pieces on the diagonal

2 TBS lemon zest (or cut outside lemon rind into thin strips)

Plum Dressing

1 tsp olive oil

1 TBS umeboshi paste

2 TBS spring water

5 large, fresh basil leaves, chopped

1 tsp lemon juice

¼ cup roasted black sesame seeds

Place 4 cups of spring water and sea salt in a saucepan and bring to boil.

Lightly blanch diakon until bright white and crispy.

Remove with a vegetable skimmer and place in a medium size bowl to cool.

Repeat with carrot matchsticks, blanch until bright orange.

Remove and place in the bowl with daikon.

Add lemon zest and set aside.

Place all ingredients for the dressing (except black sesame seeds) in a blender and blend until smooth.

Stir in roasted black sesame seeds with a spoon.

Pour over blanched salad and serve.

Tip from the Chef

This is a very refreshing salad for hot summer days. It serves up nicely on a bed of fresh lettuce. With the addition of this dressing, children tend to enjoy the flavor and taste of daikon.

KNOW YOUR INGREDIENTS - BLACK SESAME SEEDS

Black sesame seeds can be roasted and used as a garnish or ground into black sesame seed butter. They have a stronger taste than tan sesame seeds. You can purchase them already roasted or roast them yourself. To roast them yourself, use a dry cast iron or stainless steel frying pan. Make sure to rinse them first in a strainer. Stir the seeds and shake the pan often to prevent burning

Creamy Coleslaw

Yields: 4-5 servings

½ cup carrots, shredded
¼ cup purple cabbage, shredded
¾ cup green cabbage, shredded
1 TBS sea salt
1 cup tofu mayonnaise

Mix the carrot and both cabbages in a bowl.

Toss in sea salt and knead with your hands until water comes out of the vegetables.

Place in a pickle press or cover with a plate and heavy weight.

Press for 15-20 minutes or until more water comes out of the vegetables.

Open pickle press (or remove weight) and place ingredients in a colander. Rinse off excess sea salt.

Toss with tofu mayonnaise and serve.

Tofu Mayonnaise
Yields: 1 cup

1 20 oz box of silken tofu
1 tsp lemon juice
1 TBS brown rice vinegar
1 tsp mustard
1 tsp white miso

Add all ingredients into a blender and blend for approximately 4-5 minutes until creamy.

Tip from the Chef

Cabbage is hard to press unless cut very thin, which is why it is recommended to shred the cabbage for this recipe. Also, it will not give out water while being pressed unless there is enough salt and pressure. Make sure to adjust the weight (find a heavier plate and weight if necessary) and salt (add a little more) if water does not come out of the salad while it is being pressed.

KNOW YOUR INGREDIENTS - SEA SALT

Sea salt is obtained by the evaporation of seawater and unlike table salt—which is 99.5% sodium chloride—contains traces of other minerals like calcium, potassium and magnesium. A good quality sea salt should initially have a mild sweet taste when placed on the tongue. Too much salt can produce hyperactivity, aggressive behavior, increased appetite and excessive retention of water throughout the body. Too little salt can lead to lack of vitality, stagnated blood and loss of clear thinking.

Except for fresh fruit, salt should be cooked with the food, or used in pressing or pickling, instead of adding it to the dish afterwards.

Quinoa Salad

Yields: 5-6 servings

1 cup quinoa, rinsed well
2 cups of spring water
2 pinches of sea salt
¼ cup cucumber, cut into ¼-inch cubes
½ medium red onion, diced into ½-inch pieces
2 tsp umeboshi vinegar
2 tsp brown rice vinegar
½ cup parsley, chopped finely
¼ cup organic corn

Roast quinoa in cooking pot over medium heat, stirring constantly until lightly toasted and fragrant.

Add water and salt, cover pot and bring to a boil.

Simmer for 20-25 minutes.

Meanwhile, mix cucumber and onion together and add the vinegars.

When quinoa is done, turn out into a large bowl and let cool a bit.

Add parsley, cucumber/onion/vinegar mixture and organic corn to the quinoa, then mix well and serve.

Tip from the Chef

Quinoa is a little more delicate than other grains. You need to adjust your cooking temperature and water so as not to overcook it. If quinoa is overcooked, the germ or "little tail" that pops out gets disconnected from the rest of the seed and you end up with mush. Roasting it first provides a richer flavor and helps kids to enjoy the taste.

KNOW YOUR INGREDIENTS - UMEBOSHI VINEGAR

Umeboshi vinegar—though not classified as a true vinegar—can be used for pickling vegetables, in dressings, or as a substitute in any dish where you would use regular vinegars. This pale redish liquid—obtained from fermented umeboshi plums—has a salty, sour taste that adds an extra flavor dimension to food.

Tofu Mock Egg Salad

Yields: 4-5 servings

1 umeboshi plum
1 TBS white miso
2 TBS grated onion
1-14 oz container of firm tofu
2 TBS celery, chopped fine
2 TBS grated carrot
1 tsp of turmeric
(optional-for yellow coloring)

Purée umeboshi and white miso in a surabachi.

Add onion, tofu, celery and grated carrot and mash together well.

Add in turmeric for color if desired.

Serve as a garnish on a bed of lettuce and cucumber, or on a slice of bread.

Tip from the Chef

This is a wonderful replacement for egg salad. Kids love the taste!

KNOW YOUR INGREDIENTS - UMEBOSHI PLUMS

Umeboshi plums are pickled plums that aid in digestion and can be used medicinally to rid the body of many ailments such as stomach aches, sore throats and headaches that arise from an acid blood condition. Umeboshi plums are also available in a paste, which can be spread on freshly cooked corn on the cob for flavor in place of butter.

Marinated Salad

Yields: 3-4 servings

2 TBS umeboshi vinegar
2 TBS rice vinegar
1 cup cucumber, sliced thin
1 cup lotus root, sliced thin
1 cup grapes, cut in half
1 TBS roasted tan sesame seeds

Mix umeboshi and rice vinegar together in a medium size bowl.

Add cucumber, lotus root and grapes, then marinate for at least one hour.

Place into serving bowls and garnish with sesame seeds.

Tip from the Chef

Marinated vegetables must be sliced very thin in order for the marinate to soften them.

KNOW YOUR INGREDIENTS - LOTUS ROOT

The root—rhizome—of the aquatic lotus plant, *Nelumbo nucifera*, looks like a reddish-brown squash. The interior has a lace-like appearance when cut in cross section. The lotus root is slightly crunchy and mildly sweet, becoming slightly bitter as the plant matures. Lotus root helps to dissolve mucus in the body. Grated and simmered with a little spring water it helps to clear lung or sinus congestion and ease coughing.

Cucumber Wakame Salad with Sesame Seeds

Yields: 3-4 servings

1 cucumber, sliced thin

3 red radishes, sliced thin

2 strips of 3-to-4-inch pieces of dried wakame, rinsed and cut into ½-inch slices

1 TBS brown rice vinegar

¼ tsp sea salt and a pinch

2 cups of spring water

¼ cup snap peas

2 TBS roasted tan sesame seeds

Place cucumber and radish slices in a serving bowl. Mix in sea salt and let sit for 10-15 minutes.

Add vinegar and wakame and allow to sit for 10 more minutes.

Fill a small saucepan with spring water and add a pinch of sea salt.

Put on medium heat, cover and bring to boil.

Add snap peas and blanche until bright green in color.

Remove and allow to cool.

Add snap peas and roasted sesame seeds to the radish, cucumber and wakame mixture.

Toss and serve.

Tip from the Chef

This salad is extremely simple to prepare and is loaded with calcium-rich ingredients good for children's bones.

KNOW YOUR INGREDIENTS - WAKAME

Wakame is a thin, green sea vegetable that requires no soaking. Simply rinsing it with cold water makes it soft and flexible. Wakame is less salty than hiziki or arame and is very good to add daily to miso soup (no more than 1 inch per two-person serving).

Rainbow Pasta Salad

Yields: 6-7 servings

8 cups spring water

Salad Ingredients

2 cups dry tri-color rigatoni or spiral pasta
½ cup pine nuts, roasted
¼ cup black olives, cut in half
¼ cup green peppers, cut in ½ inch slices
¼ cup red peppers, cut in ½ inch slices
½ cup of brussel sprouts,
blanched in boiling water until bright in color
½ cup tofu cubes,
steamed for 5 minutes in a steamer

Salad Dressing

3 cloves of garlic, peeled and mashed
2 TBS olive oil
1 tsp lemon juice
2 tsp sea salt

Pour spring water into three-quart saucepan and bring to a boil.

Add pasta and cook for 15-20 minutes until pasta is ready.

Rinse and drain.

Arrange in a serving bowl.

Add rest of ingredients and set aside.

Mix all ingredients for the dressing in a glass jar with a lid.

Cover jar and shake to mix well.

Mix into the pasta salad.

Tip from the Chef

The pasta, tofu and vegetables need to be well seasoned due to the lemon juice in the recipe, so adjust the amount of sea salt accordingly.

KNOW YOUR INGREDIENTS - PINE NUTS

Pine nuts are edible seeds harvested from various species of pine trees. They have been used as a culinary ingredient since the Stone Age.

Raw pine nuts have a sweet, buttery flavor and a soft texture but are usually lightly toasted to enhance their flavor and add a little crunch.

Unshelled pine nuts become rancid rather quickly if they are not kept dry and refrigerated.

Fancy Fruit Salad

Yields: 4-6 servings

Salad Ingredients
½ cup blackberries
½ cup blueberries
½ cup strawberries
¼ cup green grapes
½ cup cantaloupe,
cut into melon balls
½ cup watermelon,
cut into melon balls
1 large watermelon shell,
with inside scooped out (optional)

Poppy Seed Dressing
1 TBS poppy seeds
3 TBS brown rice syrup
1 TBS lemon juice
1/8 tsp sea salt
1 TBS melon juice

Combine all ingredients for the fruit salad and place in a serving bowl.

Chill in the refrigerator while preparing the dressing.

Mix all dressing ingredients together in a small bowl, cover and store in until used.

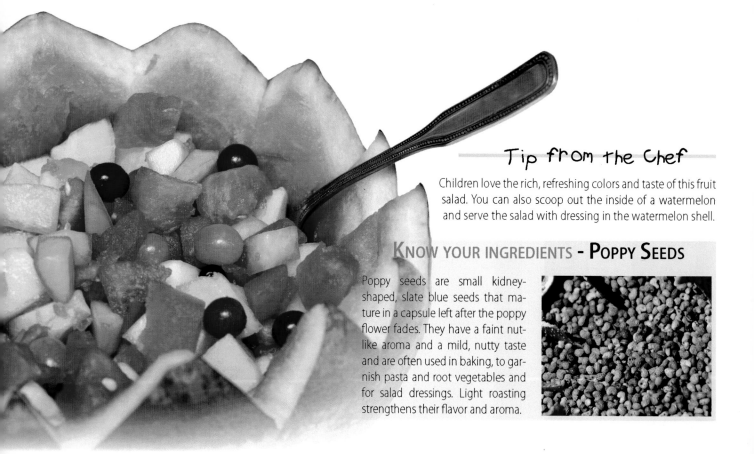

Tip from the Chef

Children love the rich, refreshing colors and taste of this fruit salad. You can also scoop out the inside of a watermelon and serve the salad with dressing in the watermelon shell.

KNOW YOUR INGREDIENTS - POPPY SEEDS

Poppy seeds are small kidney-shaped, slate blue seeds that mature in a capsule left after the poppy flower fades. They have a faint nut-like aroma and a mild, nutty taste and are often used in baking, to garnish pasta and root vegetables and for salad dressings. Light roasting strengthens their flavor and aroma.

Dream Desserts

Dulcis in fundo—a sweet finish, but a healthy one, made possible by the use of natural sweeteners like organic barley malt, organic brown rice syrup and organic maple syrup, as alternatives to processed sugar.

Even if the meal wraps up with a classic desert—cookies, cake, pie or a comforting mousse—kids can still satisfy their sweet tooth without adversely affecting their health.

The recipes that follow closely mimic these traditional favorites, but without the use of traditional unhealthy ingredients.

Making desserts with healthy ingredients and natural sweeteners means kids can truly "have their cake and eat it, too".

HEALTHY BASIC PIE CRUST

1 cup pastry flour
6 TBS extra virgin olive oil
3 TBS cold spring water

Preheat oven to 375 degrees.

Mix all ingredients together in a mixing bowl until coarsely blended, then press into a pie pan and prick inside with a fork.

Bake at 375 degrees for 15 minutes.

Variations besides those described on the facing page are: a combination of whole wheat pastry flour and spelt flour, graham flour, corn flour, brown rice flour or oat flour. For a no-flour shell, use rolled oats and ground nuts; almonds, walnuts, hazelnuts, cashews or pistachios.

Safflower or corn oil give a richer, buttery flavor. Crusts can be plain or sweetened with brown rice syrup, barley malt, maple syrup or apple juice. Try fresh carrot juice for savory pies or fruit juice, such as apple, pear or apricot, if making a sweet pie. Liquids used should be ice cold.

Almond Cream Topping
Yields: 1 ¾ cups

spring water for boiling almonds
1 cup raw almonds
¼ cup spring water
½ cup rice milk, vanilla flavor

½ cup brown rice syrup
½ tsp lemon juice
1 TBS vanilla extract
¼ tsp almond extract

Place water for boiling almonds in a large saucepan and put on medium heat, cover and bring to boil.

Add almonds and boil until skins become loose.

Remove almonds from boiling water and remove and discard all skins.

Place almonds and ¼ cup of water in a pressure cooker, then cover and cook for 90 minutes.

Turn off heat.

When the pressure comes down, remove the lid and almonds and place almonds in a food processor or blender.

Blend almonds until smooth, then add rest of ingredients and blend. If too thick, add almond cooking water to desired consistency.

Pour mixture into a bowl and place in the refrigerator to chill. As it sets, it may become too thick. Add a little water to thin out, if needed.

Lemon Pie with Almond Cream Topping

Yields: 7-8 servings

Pie Crust
(rolled thinly covers the bottom and sides of a 9" round pie pan)

1 ½ cups whole wheat pastry flour
1 cup almond meal
½ tsp sea salt
1 tsp cinnamon
4 TBS corn oil
4 TBS maple syrup

Pie Filling

3 cups of unsweetened organic apple juice
Pinch of sea salt
2 ½ TBS agar agar flakes
2 ½ TBS Kuzu, dissolved in 3 TBS spring water
¼ cup lemon juice
2 TBS grated lemon rind
1/3 cup brown rice syrup

Prepare the Pie Crust
Preheat oven to 350 degrees.

Mix dry ingredients together in a mixing bowl.

Add oil and maple syrup until mixture crumbles, yet is moist enough to press into a pie pan.

Bake pie crust in the oven for 15-20 minutes until brown.

Prepare the Pie Filling
Combine apple juice, sea salt and agar agar in a saucepan.

Place on low heat without the lid and cook until agar agar flakes dissolve (about 7-10 minutes), then turn heat off and allow to cool.

Add kuzu, stir until dissolved and reheat on low.

Continue to stir until thick and clear (approximately 7-8 minutes).

Add lemon juice, grated rind and brown rice syrup.

Pour into baked pie shell and chill.

Prepare the pie for serving
After the pie has chilled, spread Almond Cream Topping (recipe on facing page) over pie with an icing spatula.

Cut pie into slices and serve.

Tip from the Chef

Lundberg's® Sweet Dreams® Brown Rice Syrup should not be used for this recipe, as it does not allow the kuzu to thicken the pie filling.

KNOW YOUR INGREDIENTS - WHOLE WHEAT PASTRY FLOUR

Whole wheat pastry flour is finely milled, whole grain flour with a high starch and low gluten content, made from soft-white wheat. Unlike regular whole wheat flour, which makes baked goods hard and dense, the pastry variety is excellent to use in making cakes, cook-ies, muffins, pie crusts and even tempura. The pastries made with whole-wheat pastry flour will not be as light and airy as those made with white pastry flour, but they will be more nutritious because of the presence of some bran and germ.

Mello Gel-o

Yields: 1-2 servings

1 ½ cups unsweetened apple juice
Pinch of sea salt
1 TBS agar agar flakes
3 unpeeled peach slices
2 tangerine slices

Put apple juice and sea salt into a saucepan.

Add agar agar flakes.

Bring mixture to a boil and simmer on low heat until flakes dissolve. Do not stir, as the flakes will stick to the spoon.

When flakes have dissolved, pour into your favorite mold or serving bowl.

Fold in fresh fruit, or leave plain and allow to cool.

Tip from the Chef

Pure grape juice is not recommended to use in this recipe, as it prevents the agar agar flakes from gelling. Other fruit juices work well, used cold or at room temperature, as they allow the agar agar flakes to dissolve when heated.
If kept more than one day, Mello Gel-o should be stored in the refrigerator.
For variety, cook agar agar with other fruit juices or beverages such as green tea or grain coffee or spring water flavored with brown rice syrup or barley malt. Fresh or dried fruits can be added for different colors and tastes.
Vegetable aspics are great in the summer, as the agar agar has a cooling effect on the body. Try different vegetable juices or umeboshi vinegar and spring water, along with fresh scallions, carrots, cucumbers, corn and noodles or grains. Molded vegetable aspics make a beautiful presentation on a bed of salad greens.

KNOW YOUR INGREDIENTS - AGAR AGAR

Agar agar—available in bars, flakes or powder—is a white vegetarian gelatin substitute processed from various seaweeds. It is used in desserts, vegetable aspics or as a thickener for soups. Agar agar, which has a high fiber content, is a good natural laxative. Unlike regular gelatin, agar agar sets without refrigeration.

Mocha Mousse

Yields: 4-6 servings

3 TBS agar agar flakes
1/3 cup unsweetened apple juice
1 pinch of sea salt
2 cups soy milk
4 tsp grain coffee
1 tsp vanilla
5 TBS barley malt
3 TBS tahini
Roasted almonds, walnuts
or fresh fruit for garnish

Place agar agar, apple juice and sea salt in a small saucepan.

Cover and simmer for 5-8 minutes.

When agar agar flakes are dissolved, add soy milk, grain coffee, vanilla and barley malt.

Mix well and simmer for 2 minutes, then turn off the heat.

Add tahini and mix until dissolved.

Pour into bowl and refrigerate for one hour or until set.

When completely set, mix in a food processor for 1-2 minutes until smooth.

Spoon into serving bowls and chill 30 minutes to 1 hour before serving.

After mousse is chilled, garnish with roasted almonds, walnuts or fresh fruit and serve.

Tip from the Chef

For a variation, serve in tall parfait or glass dessert bowls and top with roasted almonds, walnuts or fresh strawberries for a more elegant looking dessert.

KNOW YOUR INGREDIENTS - GRAIN COFFEE

Grain coffee, which is made from roasted barley, rye, chicory and acorns, has a taste similar to lightly brewed regular coffee. Avoid those with added corn syrup, cane sugar and carob.

Blackberry Couscous Cake
with Chestnut Cream Icing

Yields: 4-5 servings

2 cups of unsweetened apple juice
2 cups of spring water
1 cup couscous
3 pinches sea salt
¼ cup fresh blackberries,
washed and drained

Tip from the Chef

For the cake: The longer you cook cous cous, the more dense and rich the cake will become.

For the Icing: You can place chestnut cream in a cake decorator to make fancy toppings or simply spread on top of the cake. Use less water if placing in a pastry bag.

Pour juice and water in a saucepan.

Add couscous and sea salt.

Bring to a boil and simmer for 30-40 minutes until the couscous is dissolved and mixture looks like cake batter. (stir often to prevent burning on the bottom of the pan).

Add blackberries, fold in and cover.

Simmer for 5-7 more minutes.

Remove from heat.

Pour mixture into a square pan and allow to cool.

Ice with Chestnut Cream.

Chestnut Cream
Yields: 1 ½ cup

2 cups of dried chestnuts,
soaked overnight

1 cup of apple juice

Pinch of sea salt
¼ cup of rice syrup
1 tsp vanilla

Place dried chestnuts, apple juice and sea salt in a pressure cooker.
Close lid, bring up to pressure and cook for 45 minutes.
Allow to cool and remove lid.
Allow to cool further and place in a blender with rice syrup and vanilla.

KNOW YOUR INGREDIENTS - DRIED CHESTNUTS

Dried chestnuts—produced by drying the nuts from the chestnut tree—contain very little fat, no cholesterol and are the only nut that contains vitamin C. When soaked, pressure cooked and mashed they create a sweet paste used for dessert fillings and frostings. Chestnuts should be stored in airtight bags, or containers free of moisture.

Hocus Pocus Crispy Treats

Yields: 6-8 servings

1 cup barley malt
1 cup organic peanut butter
½ cup roasted unsalted organic peanuts
3 cups crispy brown rice cereal

Place barley malt and peanut butter in a medium-size saucepan.

Turn heat to low and stir until creamy (about 3-4 minutes).

Remove from heat and set aside.

In a mixing bowl, fold together peanuts and crispy brown rice cereal.

Add heated barley malt/peanut butter mixture.

Stir to coat mixture well.

Wet hands and form into 1-inch balls or press lightly into shallow square pan.

If in a pan, allow to set until firm before slicing.

AS SEEN ON:

Tip from the Chef

Hocus Pocus Crispy Treats are similar to marshmallow treats, without the added processed sugar. Any nut or nut butter can be added in place of the peanuts and peanut butter. Brown rice syrup or maple syrup can be substituted for the barley malt. For variety, add dried fruits, coconut, cinnamon, vanilla and roasted seeds. Keep heat low and stir constantly when heating sweeteners, as they burn easily.

KNOW YOUR INGREDIENTS - CRISPY BROWN RICE

Crispy brown rice cereal is made from cooking and puffing whole brown rice ker-

nels—one of the only cereals still manufactured without added cane sugar

Ginger Snap Cookies

Yields: 18 cookies

¾ cup oat flour
½ cup almond meal/flour
½ tsp baking powder
¼ tsp sea salt
1 tsp ground ginger
½ tsp mace
¼ cup safflower oil
½ tsp vanilla
¼ cup rice syrup
¼ cup maple syrup

Pre-heat the oven to 325 degrees.

Cover 2 baking trays with parchment paper and set aside.

Place the dry ingredients into a bowl and mix.

Place the oil, vanilla, rice syrup and maple syrup in a second bowl and whisk together.

Add the wet ingredients to the dry and mix gently to form a batter.

Place a tablespoon of cookie batter for each cookie on the sheets. Leave a good amount of space between each cookie because they spread.

Bake in the oven for 15 minutes. These cookies bake quickly so you may want to check after 12 minutes.

Allow to cool before removing from the sheets.

Tip from the Chef

Commercial ginger snaps are usually made with a lot of refined-white sugar. To modify regular recipes: use 1 1/3 cups of rice syrup and reduce liquid in recipes by ¼ cup. The cookies will still have a sweet taste and a crunchy texture, but wll not have the ill-effects of white sugar.

KNOW YOUR INGREDIENTS - SAFFLOWER OIL

Safflower oil—obtained by pressing the seeds of the safflower plant, *Carthamus tinctorius*—is a nearly colorless, mild tasting vegetable oil well-suited for recipes in which a pronounced oil flavor is not desired. Safflower oil comes in two varieties—refined mono- unsaturated and unrefined polyunsaturated—each with very distinct uses. The monounsaturated variety has a high-smoke point making it ideal for deep frying and sautéing, while the polyunsaturated variety, which becomes rancid when heated, is used as a cold carrier oil.

Bewitching Beverages

Beverages have many functions in a macrobiotic diet besides providing the necessary hydration of our bodies: they can aid digestion after a meal, provide remedies for minor ailments, boost our energy naturally and just simply delight our taste buds. In fact, because of the high water content of plants, following a plant-based macrobiotic diet means your water intake will already be rather elevated even without consuming beverages.

Beverages should be served warm, or at room temperature to ease digestion, which is why a cup of warm tea is an ideal drink for after a meal.

Macrobiotic teas—which are mild tasting and contain no added stimulants, such as caffeine—are an excellent choice as the principle beverage for kids of all ages. They can be prepared either unsweetened or sweetened with grain syrups or fruit juices. Remedy teas can also be produced from foods used in macrobiotic cooking.

Natural spring water, which is the basis for nearly all of the recipes that follow, is the best choice for an all-purpose beverage.

Amasake drink and fruit and vegetable juices can be used to create beverages that are not only healthy, but are also delicious taste treats that kids will find irresistible.

Tasty Tea
Basic Recipe for Macrobiotic Tea

Yields: 3-4 cups

1 quart spring water
2 TBS of loose tea or one tea bag

Pour spring water into a teapot and bring to a boil.

Reduce the heat to low.

Place the tea bag or the loose tea into the pot (or into a tea ball, then into the pot).

Simmer for 3 to 5 minutes.

If loose tea was used, strain through a tea strainer when serving.

Leave remaining tea on the stove and reheat when needed.

Serve with a twist of lemon peel or mix with some unsweetened apple juice, if desired.

Tip from the Chef

Prevent bitterness by not boiling tea. Change the simmer time—less time for lighter tea or more time for darker tea. If using loose tea, leave in the pot and use once more for a slightly weaker tea. For a stronger flavor, add 1 teaspoon of fresh loose tea. Follow directions above and adjust amounts to make roasted barley, roasted brown rice or mu teas or grain coffee.

KNOW YOUR INGREDIENTS - BANCHA TEA

Bancha tea is a popular macrobiotic tea from Japan that is late-harvested from the *Camellia sinensis* plant. Bancha leaves are often slightly roasted to make Hojicha, a toasty, slightly caramel-flavored tea, low in caffeine. The stems, stalks and twigs of the plant are also roasted to make Kukicha, which has a sweeter flavor and even less caffeine. Both are very different than commercial teas, as they are alkalizing instead of acidic to the body and therefore, aid in digestion.

Lotus Root Tea

Yields: 1 cup

½ cup of finely grated lotus root
1 TBS spring water
1 pinch of sea salt
or 2 drops of shoyu

Squeeze juice from the grated lotus root into a small sauce pan.

Add spring water.

Put on low heat and simmer for 10 minutes.

Add a pinch of sea salt or a few drops of shoyu.

Serve warm.

As seen on:

Tip from the Chef

To obtain the most juice from the lotus root, use a fine porcelain ceramic grater to grate the lotus root. If you are unable to find fresh lotus root, look for powdered instant lotus root tea.

Know your ingredients - Lotus Root

Lotus root is very low in saturated fat, rich in dietary fiber and vitamins C, B2 (riboflavin), B6 and thiamin. Tea made from lotus root helps dissolve mucus in the body and relieve coughing and congestion.

Amasake Fruit Shakes

Yields: 3-4 servings

1 cup fresh strawberries (or other fresh fruit)
1 cup amasake drink (vanilla flavored)

Place strawberries in a blender.

Pour the amasake drink on top of the berries.

Blend until smooth.

Pour into glasses, garnish with a strawberry and serve.

Tip from the Chef

Choose your flavor of amasake drink and your favorite fruit. These are much more digestible than soy shakes or other smoothies. When using amasake drink, no other liquid needs to be added.

KNOW YOUR INGREDIENTS - AMASAKE DRINK

Amasake drink, available in a variety of flavors—is a traditional Japanese beverage made by combining amasake with water, heating to simmer and  serving garnished with grated ginger. Amasake—an ancient Japanese sweetener with a creamy texture and malty taste—is made from fermented rice.

Cereal Grain Milk

Yields: 3-4 servings

1 cup short-grain brown rice
soaked overnight in 1 ¼ cups of spring water

¾ cup sweet brown rice
soaked overnight in 1 cup of spring water

¼ cup barley
soaked overnight in ½ cup spring water

3 additional cups spring water
1-inch piece of kombu
2 tsp of brown rice syrup or barley malt
4-inch square piece of cheesecloth

Place all grains with soaking water in large pressure cooker, then add 3 additional cups of spring water.

Add kombu, then cover and place on medium heat.

Once up to pressure, lower heat and cook for 1 ½ hours.

Turn off heat, allow pressure valve to lower and remove lid.

Remove kombu and strain through cheesecloth to remove the bran.

Sweeten with brown rice syrup or barley malt.

Tip from the Chef

Brown rice can be used alone for this recipe or millet and oats can be substituted for sweet rice and barley. A teaspoon of crushed roasted, sesame seeds can be cooked with the grains for added nutrition and taste.

This formula can be made thicker for older children by adding more grain, or thinned out for newborn babies by adding enough spring water to serve through a baby bottle.

The mixture can be refrigerated for up to two days and then reheated.

Cereal grain milk can be given to babies if the mother cannot breast feed. Since whole grains are so nutritionally balanced, macrobiotic grain milk is a wonderful alternative to baby formula and a great replacement for store-purchased instant baby porridges.

KNOW YOUR INGREDIENTS - SPRING WATER

Spring water is natural, untreated water from underground aquifers. Most spring waters contain traces of minerals that have dissolved in the water as it moved through underground rocks and—depending on the nature of the geology—some even be-come effervescent as the result of natural carbonation during this passage. The minerals dissolved in spring water give it a slight taste and a slightly alkaline ph.

Unlike most tap water, spring water does not contain additives like chlorine or fluoride.

Sweet Vegetable Drink

Yields: 3-4 servings

4 cups spring water
¼ cup finely chopped onions
¼ cup finely chopped carrots
¼ cup finely chopped cabbage
¼ cup finely chopped sweet winter squash
(butternut, buttercup or Hokkaido)

Place spring water in a medium-size saucepan.

Cover and bring to a boil.

Add onions and return to a boil.

Turn heat down to simmer for 2-3 minutes, without the lid.

Add rest of ingredients, then cover pan and return to boil on medium heat.

Reduce heat to low and simmer for 20 minutes.

Strain the vegetables from the broth with a vegetable skimmer.

Serve the broth in tea cups, either hot, or at room temperature.

Tip from the Chef

Sweet vegetable drink may be kept in the refrigerator for up to 2 days, but should be warmed again, or allowed to return to room temperature before drinking.

Sweet vegetable drink is good for hypoglycemia. It softens pancreatic tightness caused by heavy animal food consumption. It provides a steady even flow of blood sugar and helps to relax the body and muscles. A small cup daily, or every other day, especially in the afternoon, helps satisfy the desire for sweets and reduces the cravings children often have for simple sugars and other stronger sweets.

KNOW YOUR INGREDIENTS - WINTER SQUASH

Winter squash are warm-season vegetables that belong to the *Cucurbitaceae* (gourds, melons) family of plants and come in a variety of species, each with a unique taste. Unlike summer squash, which are harvested immature with their rind still tender, winter squash are harvested when they are fully mature and their skins have hardened into a tough rind. By al-lowing the squash to mature to this stage, they can be stored for use throughout the winter—hence the name "winter squash".

Butternut and buttercup squash, with their sweet, nutty flavor, are the most popular of the winter squash, though the chestnut flavored Japanese Hokkaido squash, is gaining a strong following. Winter squash are often pureed and used in soups, casseroles and in baking.

Lemonade
Yields: 4-5 glasses

Juice from 5 fresh organic lemons   4 TBS brown rice syrup
1 quart spring water   2-3 sprigs of mint

Place freshly squeezed lemon juice in a pitcher.
Fill to the top with spring water.
Stir in brown rice syrup until dissolved.
Pour into glasses, garnish with sprigs of mint and serve.

Tip from the Chef

Other fresh fruit juices can be substituted for the lemon juice. If you choose another fruit juice, adjust the amount of brown rice syrup according to taste.

Abracadabra Energy Drink
Yields: 3-4 servings

1 quart of spring water   3 umeboshi plums

Fill medium saucepan or tea pot with spring water.
Add umeboshi plums.
Cover and bring to boil.
Lower heat and simmer for 30 minutes.
Cool and pour into glasses to serve.

Tip from the Chef

Reduce the number of plums for small children as plums contain a lot of salt.

Carrot Juice
Yields: 3-4 servings

3-4 medium size carrots   1 organic green apple

Juice all ingredients with a vegetable juicer.
Pour into individual glasses and serve at room temperature.

Tip from the Chef

If you do not own a juicer, you can finely grate the ingredients and squeeze out the juice or purchase organic carrot juice plain, or mixed with other juices.
Other delicious combinations of vegetable juices include carrot/red apple, carrot/orange and ginger juice, carrot/celery, carrot/beet juice, carrot/leafy greens juice or simply plain leafy greens juice

Lunches & Snacks:

Healthful Items to Pack for School Children

Chapter 5

Healthy eating begins at home, but it does not end there. When your children leave for school, make sure that health-promoting lunches and snacks leave with them. Replace starchy white bread and flour products with whole grains and whole wheat bread. Whole grains and cracked grains are the most nutritious; whole grain breads and pastas are a nice addition.

Plan lunch with a healthy idea in mind. If you don't see to it that your children eat a nourishing lunch, who will? It's best not to trust your children's health and well-being to school cafeterias, where convenience and cost effectiveness, rather than balanced-meal planning often carry the day—and the menu.

Strategies to Promote Better Lunches and Snacks

Keep it colorful—a lunch that is bright and full of color is appealing to eat.

Keep it fresh—prepare food in the evening and pack it in containers that will keep it well-preserved. Plastic containers from takeout food make fine containers. Remember to wrap foods individually and to pack a cool pack during hot days to keep food fresh.

Make lunch fun—provide colorful wrappers, bags, containers and thermoses.

Make it easy—leftovers from dinner are fine if you enjoy them.

Keep it simple—kids don't have much time to eat, so downsize the super size. Choose proportions that best suit individual needs.

Go for variety—don't repeat too many of the same sandwich and snack items during the week.

Go organic when possible—organic foods make a huge difference in your health.

Read food labels—ingredients on those labels are listed in descending order by volume, so pay close attention to the first two or three ingredients because they often make up the bulk of a particular food. Make sure they're healthy, then look for chemicals and/or additives among the rest of the items on the label. Better yet, choose foods that say "no artificial flavors or colors and no additives" on the package.

Become a food critic—don't believe everything you see and hear on television. Food marketers' main goal is to make money by enticing people to purchase their products. Thus, food advertisements are not always created with your health in mind.

Drink water or fruit juice—they are much better for you than sugary drinks and sodas.

Advocate for healthy eating—do your best to make a difference in your children's school cafeteria, classroom activities and other events.

PACKING A HEALTHY SCHOOL LUNCH - SANDWICH IDEAS

Outside

- Whole wheat bread
- Whole wheat pita bread
- Sourdough bread
- Corn bread
- Wraps (spinach, red pepper, whole wheat)
- Corn tortillas
- Corn or rice cakes
- Matzo
- Flatbreads
- Sprouted breads

Inside Fillings

- Hummus
- Bean spreads
- Veggie burger
- Seitan—can be fried with onions
- Tofu—fried, scrambled, or as a packaged spread
- Tempeh—fried or simmered in shoyu
- Vegetarian refried beans and brown rice
- Grilled veggies
- Grilled Portobello mushroom
- Nut butters without added sugar and oils—peanut, almond, soy and hazelnut
- Seed Butters—sesame tahini, sunflower seed and pumpkin seed
- Jellies—no added sugar

- Fruit or vegetable spreads—apple, pear, peach, or pumpkin butter
- Fakin Bacon

Toppings

- Organic dill pickles
- Organic sauerkraut
- Ketchup—sugar-free
- Mustard—sugar-free mustard and sauerkraut can be added to fried seitan or tofu
- Tofu mayonnaise—sugar-free
- Roasted red peppers
- Stir fried or grilled veggies
- Fried onions
- Melted mochi
- Soy cheese
- Organic olives
- Finely chopped carrots, cucumbers, lettuce, tomato

PACKING A HEALTHY SCHOOL LUNCH - SNACK & DRINK IDEAS

Smooth Snacks

- Sugar-free apple or pear sauce
- Soymilk or amasake pudding plain or mixed with fruit
- Soy yogurts

Sweet Snacks

- Dried fruits (raisins, apples, peaches, apricots)
- Fruit roll ups
- Low-fat fruit juice or grain syrup sweetened cookies and muffins
- Sugar-free graham crackers
- Organic sugar-free canned fruit
- Granola (sweetened with maple syrup or grain sweeteners)
- Organic fruit leather
- Homemade baked goods using maple syrup or grain sweeteners

Dry or Salty Snacks

- Roasted sunflower seeds, pumpkin seeds; avoid giving whole nuts to young children
- Organic popcorn, air popped, seasoned with olive oil, sesame seeds and sea salt
- Sugar-free dried cereal such as fruit-juice-flavored corn-flakes, i.e., Oatios
- Brown Rice Crispies (sugar and chemical free)
- Trail mix, fruit juice or grain sweetened
- Low-salt, low-fat, whole grain crackers
- Low-salt, low-fat, whole grain pretzels
- Low-fat grain tortilla chips or potato chips

Warm Snacks

- Vegetable or Miso Soups
- Hot grain cereals
- Vegetarian refried beans in tortilla
- Baked squash or pumpkin
- Grain salads (rice, couscous, bulgur, etc.)
- Mochi (pounded sweet rice, plain or cinnamon raisin)
- Vegetarian chili
- Corn on the cob
- Veggie sushi
- Lightly boiled vegetables

Cool and Refreshing Snacks

- Pasta salads
- Couscous salads
- Raw vegetables: carrot, celery, daikon, red or green peppers, cucumber, zucchini with a prepared dip*
- Raw salad with dressing** packed in separate container
- Fresh fruit salad from grapes, strawberries, orange, apple, raspberries, blueberries, melon
- Watermelon cut into pieces

- Apple, pear, orange, tangerine, or melon slices
- Applesauce (unsweetened)
- Sugar-free sherbets
- Fruit-juice popsicles
- Mello Jell-O (see recipe on page 88)

Drinks

- Boxed juices without any chemical additives, sugars, or preservatives
- Smoothies made from amasake, fruit juice and fresh fruit blended together
- Boxed rice or soy milk
- Carbonated fruit drinks without added sugars

*Dressing for raw vegetable and fruit dishes: tofu dip, hummus, bean dip, seed and nut butters
**Dressings can be made from the following ingredients: balsamic, brown rice, or umeboshi vinegar, tahini, orange or lemon juice, salt, olive or sesame oil, mustard and shoyu

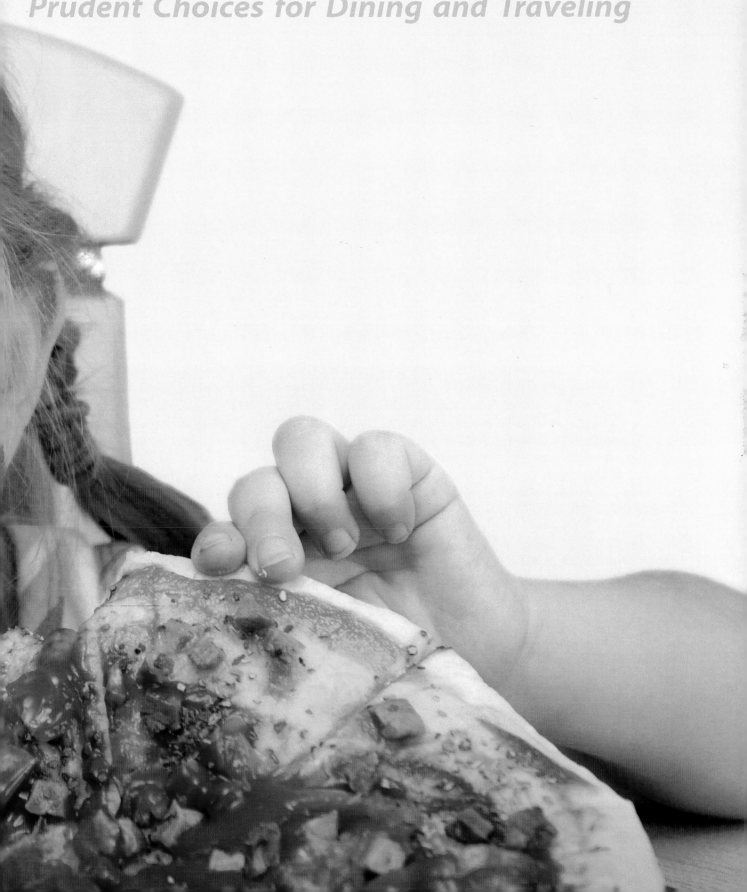

Magic to Go
Prudent Choices for Dining and Traveling

Chapter 6

The more you practice eating well, the more you will become aware of the vast number of restaurants serving foods that are simply designed to fill your belly while not providing you with balanced, nutritious meals. These restaurants are numerous and sadly, are the only kind available in many parts of the country. Often their foods are genetically engineered, commercially preserved and machine made. Consequently, the magical, healing food properties are gone by the time they reach your plate.

To continue on our enlightened path of healing through foods, we must remain conscious eaters and pay close attention to restaurants that rock! Vegan restaurants, health food stores with cafes and ethnic restaurants are the best bet—or restaurants that simply take pride in serving organic, vegan products and rely more on hands-on food production rather than machine-made dishes.

Chinese, Japanese, Mexican, Italian, Thai, Vietnamese, Middle Eastern and other ethnic restaurants offer some nice vegetarian and grain dishes. In addition, these kinds of restaurants often prepare food with thoughtful care. Homemade foods from another culture—created from grains, vegetables, sea vegetables, beans and fruits—are often the most delicious and satisfying. And, if you ever have the opportunity to travel to another country and try their cuisine first hand, you will be amazed.

In your culinary travels, see if you can taste the time, effort and thought that went into creating your dish. See if you can tell if the chef considered the natural principals of balancing tastes, textures, smells and color. Do you feel completely satisfied after completing the meal, or do you crave more? Chefs from other cultures often know how to balance dishes and meals naturally. You can be inspired by tasting their creations and getting new cooking ideas for yourself.

Look for restaurants that carry less processed foods and are more conscientious about the quality of their food, advocating the use of plant-based ingredients. If you run out of choices of restaurants while traveling, head for the nearest salad bar, where you can often find fresh vegetables and sometimes beans and grains.

Become a wizard at menu reading. Know good-quality ingredients when you see them. Make wise choices. Ask your waiter or waitress for more information if you have any questions about a dish. Become Sally in the movie *When Harry Met Sally* when she bends the ear of her waiter while ordering her meal.

Ask about the soup base. Is it chicken stock? Do sauces and dressings contain meat, dairy products, or sugar. Ask for vegan options that the chef can prepare.

Here are some key items to look for on the menus of restaurants that rock! Some menus will highlight them for you by labeling them as healthy for your heart, sugar free, dairy free, vegetarian, or vegan.

Key Items in Restaurants that Rock

Cooked beans—cooked in water or vegetable broth, not lard or chicken broth! Sometimes Mexican restaurants offer refried beans vegetarian style.

Vegetable and grain soups—cooked with vegetable broth, not chicken broth, as a base.

Rice (brown, white, or risotto)—cooked in water, not chicken broth.

Brown rice sushi—rolled without sugar or chemicals.

Sautéed, steamed, or boiled vegetables—served without butter. Some of the most unlikely restaurants may offer these in omelets at breakfast. Just tell them you want the vegetables steamed without the eggs!

Salads—without dressing or with an oil-and-vinegar dressing on the side.

Corn on the cob—without butter.

Steamed vegetables with tofu—without MSG or sugar.

Japanese noodles—udon or soba noodles in broth without fish or egg in the broth.

Homemade bread—the best choice is sourdough without a lot of added sweeteners.

Oatmeal—without sugar or milk.

TRAVELING WITH YOUR FOOD

Traveling is very yang (constricting and tightening to the body) especially long travel on airplanes. Avoid hard-baked flour products and sweets and stick to light, fresh vegetable and grain dishes. Purchase a large-mouth stainless thermos and bring your own home cooked food as much as possible. Rice balls, rice and veggie sushi, green rolls and blanched veggies will keep you feeling light and refreshed during your trip.

Check out our suggestions for lunches and snacks in Chapter 5 and remember some of these easy-to-pack foods:

- Roasted nuts and seeds
- Dried fruit (without sulfites)
- Trail mix (without sugar)
- Unsweetened apple sauce
- Wraps or other sandwiches on whole grain breads
- Juice boxes
- Sugar-free cookies
- Popcorn
- Celery with a peanut spread inside
- Rice syrup candies
- Toasted nori
- Ume plums (a pinch of plum can help eliminate a headache, stomach ache, or sore throat)
- Fresh fruit

Tempura vegetables—ask for vegetable tempura instead of shrimp tempura and ask if the oil used for frying is vegetable based. The best-quality tempura is made from fresh vegetables instead of frozen.

Pasta—whole grain or semolina without egg served with olive oil and garlic or marinara sauce.

Corn grits or polenta—without butter and cheese.

Tofu scramble—if you can find it.

Muffins, cookies, pies and cakes—dairy, sugar and fat free.

Pancakes or waffles—with real maple syrup; skip the powdered sugar on top.

Pizza—with a whole-grain crust, but without cheese.

Vegetarian Mexican tacos, chips and burritos—cooked in vegetable oil, not lard.

French fries or onion rings—cooked in vegetable oil.

Veggie burgers—these come in all sizes and shapes and may be made from beans, grains, potatoes, mushrooms, tofu and textured vegetable protein.

Tempeh burgers—usually better in quality than veggie burgers because food companies are not familiar enough with tempeh yet to add a slew of additives.

Baked potato—without the sour cream, butter and bacon.

Enjoy your Day Off from Cooking

Grab your restaurant guide and head for the healthiest meal you can find and remember these helful dining suggestions:

- Choose good-quality restaurants as much as possible.
- Consider choosing ethnic food.
- Call ahead of time and speak to the hostess or chef about the possibility of having a grain or vegetable dish prepared.
- Politely ask the wait staff smart food questions.
- Review the menu and look for our food suggestions listed above.
- Memorize the sentence: "No meat, dairy, or sugar please."

Fresh fruit—organic if possible.

Falafel—a fried ball or patty made of spiced field beans or chickpeas, which dates back to Biblical times. Try our falafel recipe first (page 59), then see how it compares to that served in a Middle Eastern or vegetarian restaurant.

Hummus—the best-quality is made from chickpeas, shoyu, lemon juice and sometimes garlic. Some restaurants serve hummus with a layer of oil floating on top—which is more difficult to digest and may leave you with a stomach ache—so be sure to ask your server to hold the oil.

KITCHEN TRAVEL KIT

When traveling for a length of time, it's ideal to find lodgings with a kitchen and a gas stove—or at least a kitchenette with a hotplate—located close to a health food store or produce market. This will help you keep the refrigerator stocked with nutritious, organic produce. If you do not have a refrigerator available, bring along a cooler in which you can keep food cold with ice. Carry along this travel-kitchen kit with convenient kitchen equipment, seasonings and condiments to recreate your magic!

- Small electric rice cooker/pressure cooker or saucepan
- Wooden spoons
- Small cutting board and knife
- Grater
- Quick-cooking grains such as rolled oats, couscous and bulgur wheat
- Quick-cooking beans such as red lentils and split peas
- Kuzu
- Agar agar
- Seasonings—umeboshi plums, shoyu, sea salt, umeboshi vinegar, brown rice vinegar, sesame oil, miso paste
- Dried fruit and raisins
- Roasted seeds and nuts
- Wakame, kombu and nori
- Apple juice

- Brown rice syrup or barley malt
- Loaf of un-yeasted sourdough bread
- Fruit jam without any added sugar
- Nut butter
- Mochi
- Tofu
- Noodles of any kind, especially ramen, which are quick and easy to prepare
- Soy/rice milk and dried cereal
- Hot breakfast cereals such as corn grits and oatmeal
- Whole grain waffle and pancake mix (without added sugar) and maple syrup
- Thermos, to keep food hot
- Prepared foods from your favorite takeout place to complement your meal the first night

Tabouli—usually found in Middle Eastern restaurants or salad bars, tabouleh is made from cracked grain and a variety of other ingredients including fresh mint, fresh parsley, chopped tomatoes, onion, extra virgin olive oil, lemon juice, salt and pepper.

Couscous—this tiny-grained pasta is made from ground semolina flour. There are three types of couscous: whole wheat, white and Israeli, which is much larger than other varieties of couscous.

Cold breakfast cereal—without sugar served with soy or rice milk is the best choice. I recommend Erewhon Crispy Brown Rice Original® and New Morning Raisin Bran® as they do not have added cane sugar.

Apple butter—your best bet for a spread. Unlike commercial jam, it is usually made without added sugar.

Jellies or Jams—without added sugar.

And for Drinks Keep It Simple!

Hot water—bring your own tea bags.

Fruit juice—unsweetened.

Spring water—use fresh spring or filtered water for drinking and cooking. Too much tap water is polluted with added fluorides and chemicals.

Homestyle Meals

Nutrition Tips for Parents and Schools

Chapter 7

The general health of American school children has been declining steadily for some time now. According to the American Heart Association, close to five million children ages six through seventeen are seriously overweight, a number that has more than tripled in the past twenty years. The number of obese twelve- to seventeen-year-olds has risen more than 30 percent since the 1970s, while the number of obese six- to eleven-year-olds has risen 54 percent.

Along with obesity, all sorts of health problems are on the rise for children: cancer, early onset diabetes, allergies, ADD (Attention Deficit Disorder) and heart disease to name a few. Efforts to solve these problems through dieting and exercise have been largely unsuccessful and the incidents of health problems continues to increase.

Consuming large amounts of sugar and fat is obviously not helping the situation. We really need to ask ourselves if we want our children to continue down this path of unhealthy eating, a path that will ultimately produce an adult population afflicted with serious health issues.

It is unrealistic to expect schoolchildren to expend the effort necessary to follow a healthy diet on their own. They need our help. Children are so easily tempted to choose unhealthy convenience foods, often because they are surrounded by them and are not educated well enough to make better choices. Parents more often than not are pressed for time and rely too much on quick convenience foods for feeding their families. What is needed is an innovative approach to eating that recognizes the parameters of modern life.

We must make it a priority to feed our children well and we must start in the home and at school. We as parents owe it to our children to serve as healthy role models and to encourage daily smart food choices. Meals eaten at home and school should be nutritious and delicious.

Our president is currently on a campaign to fight the obesity issue by advocating the reduction of large food portions in restaurants and encouraging kids to get plenty of exercise. Public school districts are now required to form policy committees to address obesity issues as well. This is not enough, however.

Many food manufacturers and the media are working against us. While conscientious parents and educators try to give children messages about healthy eating, the media provides even more messages of the opposite kind. Food manufacturers know that children naturally prefer sweet-tasting food and that they are attracted to brightly packaged food with toys inside, so they continue to market all sorts of gimmicks to our children. Some parents eventually fall into the trap of rewarding children with candy and sweets when they behave well, so naturally children become familiar with sweets and continue to crave more of them over time.

According to the Center for Science in the Public Interest, two-thirds of the commercials on Saturday morning television are food commercials. Ninety-five percent of those commercials promote fast foods and junk foods, which are high in fat, sugar and salt.

Bringing the Magical Healing to School Lunches

- Tasting parties, held in the cafeteria and classrooms, that feature wholesome, organic, non-processed snack, lunch and breakfast entrée items.
- Classroom visits by food service personnel, nutritionists and community members to educate students about nutritious foods from other cultures.
- Increase cafeteria managers' awareness of the USDA food program list of healthy commodity items and suggest they teach their workers how to prepare these items in a healthy way.
- Initiate theme days in the cafeteria that focus on foods of different cultures, supported by classroom education.
- Provide students with a formal dining experience—complete with tablecloths, invited guests and good quality food—once a week.
- Develop a school garden of edible plants that are used in cooking classes.
- Support nutrition education programs for all staff, including teachers, administrators and cafeteria workers.

What Is a Parent to Do?

For starters, monitor television watching and begin to look at what your child is eating at home and at school. Many children don't eat well because they are not familiar with the taste, texture and smell of healthy food. Slowly begin to introduce your children to the new tastes, colors and smells of wholesome, organic foods. Create new dishes from our recipes in *Macro Magic for Kids*. Invite your children into the kitchen to help prepare a meal with you; and if you have time, introduce your children to a vegetable garden. Explain to them how plants grow and how they transform sunshine and rain into chlorophyll—and how this ultimately nourishes our blood cells.

Teach your children the value of eating well and before they go off to school, make sure to pack some healthy lunch and snack items for them (see Chapter 5). Get your children into the habit of eating smart!

Why Aren't Schools Feeding Children Better?

Currently most school lunches contain no whole grain, fresh fruits, or vegetables. In fact, too many students opt for the snack line and fill up on artificial, sugar-filled, processed foods. Often the only foods they consume in a day are those loaded with sugar and fat.

Most school lunch programs get little or no local funding. Schools are left to rely on profits from their own food sales, which are usually minimal in price, to cover their own costs. Pressure is placed on them to create meals that are cost effective to prepare, that appeal to children and that meet federal guidelines. Often when they do find a cost-effective, healthy food it is not familiar to children—and thus not appealing to them—sales decline.

Even if a school finds a product that is health promoting, cost effective and flavorful, adopting it is more complicated than making a simple menu change. Training cafeteria staff to prepare new foods and educating pupils and parents takes time and money.

PARENTS: WORK YOUR MAGIC IN THE KITCHEN

➥ Plan menus ahead of time while keeping health in mind. Add a healthy soup, grain, or vegetable dish as often as possible to your meals.

➥ Learn one new recipe a week from this book and add it to your standard menu choices. You will surprise yourself with how successful you will become at working the magic!

➥ Make grain and bean dishes in advance. Cook a large amount of either grains or beans to use in soups, wraps or stews throughout the week.

➥ Think "grain and greens balance a meal." Remember always to complement a grain dish with a vegetable dish, especially some freshly cooked greens.

➥ Find the closest market that carries good-quality organic produce and replenish your supply as needed. Explore the areas where you work, live, or travel in order to find the best-quality produce and prepared foods.

➥ Make or buy nutritious snacks to take the edge off family members' hunger when they come to the kitchen.

➥ Have a family member help you prepare one item he or she can bring to the table proudly.

➥ Inspire friends and neighbors to prepare and share healthy meals.

➥ Keep a list of quick, easy and nutritious recipes such as noodles and broth, stir-fried dishes, veggie wraps and one-dish meals.

➥ Learn to use leftovers creatively. Leftover grains and beans can be turned easily into stir fries, fillings for wraps, stews and soups.

➥ Take cooking classes to stay inspired with new ideas.

➥ Learn the principle of yin and yang and practice it daily. Know when you or your family members need warming foods (yang) or cooling foods (yin) to create more strength (yang) or more relaxation (yin).

➥ Don't eat if you are not hungry and don't force feed your kids. Sleep is often the best remedy when people are overworked and stressed.

➥ Avoid being a short order cook and trying to keep up with the likes and dislikes of everyone in your family. Introduce one dish and see how everyone responds. Remember the dish if they like it well and repeat it.

➥ Allow family members to monitor their own portions, keeping in mind two rules of thumb: eat until you feel satisfied but not full; avoid eating or drinking three hours before bedtime.

➥ Keep on hand quick-cooking, healthy ingredients such as ramen, mochi, grain burgers, cans of beans, quick-cooking rice, tempeh, sourdough bread, sandwich fillings, tofu and a variety of vegetables that can be steamed or stir-fried.

➥ Keep your kitchen organized, with cooking utensils and seasonings close to the stove.

➥ Incorporate some good-quality take-out items from a natural food store in your area.

➥ Cook breakfast in the evening. While washing the dishes from the dinner meal, cook a pot of oatmeal or other hot cereal grain on the stove. After cooking, cover the pot with a sushi mat overnight. In the morning reheat and serve.

➥ Prepare miso soup on a regular basis. Its healing properties are outstanding and it's a wonderful dish for all family members to have daily. Remember to make it less salty for children younger than ten.

➥ Bring some of your own sugar-free baked items to birthday parties and other activities where food is served. If you do not have time to bake, find a health-conscious bakery or ask your present baker to consider using whole grain flours and to substitute barley malt, rice syrup, or maple syrup for sugar.

➥ Be creative and to think about tastes and color!

Every little effort helps to create a change. I recommend the following steps be taken:

1. Require that schools offer only healthy, nutrient-dense meals on a daily basis, so that children have no choice but to eat a healthy meal. This includes offering varied hot vegetarian meals daily.
2. Provide schools with more fresh fruits and vegetables, including calcium-rich vegetables and less meat, poultry and fried foods as part of the commodity foods program.
3. Mandate that non-dairy beverages such as unsweetened fruit juice, soymilk, or rice milk be offered daily as a milk alternative, whether or not a medical or dietary need is shown.

In order for a school lunch program to be successful, it must begin introducing new healthy food items on the menu daily because children tend to choose foods that are not only familiar to them but are also most available. We know that it takes a number of exposures to a new food before children become familiar with it.

Pathways to Healthy Eating Habits

In addition to being provided with healthy food items daily, kids need to be given the opportunity to learn why these foods are beneficial to their health. Information about the Department of Agriculture's new food pyramid, about how to read food labels and to make appropriate choices and how food affects the health of one's body should be taught continually in our schools—in the classroom as well as the cafeteria.

Hands-on organic gardening and cooking classes in how to prepare grains, beans, vegetables and fruits seem to produce the most success in educating children about healthy eating. Children familiar with growing and cooking these foods will be more motivated to taste them and to continue eating them on a regular basis than will children who do not. The latter will often spend their time removing broccoli and carrots from their pasta salads at lunch time.

Parents should volunteer to serve on a school nutrition committee or policy board. These are being developed in schools across the country. Parents also should advocate for the steps listed above—as well as for other initiatives—by speaking to their school administrators. Parents, become a voice. Remember that the squeaky wheel is often heard.

HEALTH-PROMOTING FOOD EXCHANGES
Substitute the following health-promoting foods for less-healthy ingredients in your present recipes.

Out with the old	In with the new
milk	soymilk, rice milk, oat milk, almond milk
cheese, cream sauces, or eggs	tofu
red meat, chicken, pork	seitan or tempeh
butter	olive oil (especially nice on popcorn)
egg or cornstarch thickeners	kuzu
jello	agar agar flakes
sugar	barley malt, brown rice syrup, or maple syrup
baking soda, yeast, or egg leavening agents	baking powder
soda	sparkling fruit juice
herbal teas	twig or roasted grain teas
commercial salt	roasted seeds, gomasio seasoning mix, nuts

Recipe Index